COOKING FOR LIFE

by Gordon and Laura Tessler

Published by
Be Well Publications

© Copyright 1995

All Rights Reserved by Gordon S. Tessler.

Permission to reproduce material contained in this book must be obtained in writing from the publisher.

For information contact:

Be Well Publications

P.O. Box 99005

Raleigh, North Carolina 27624

Printed in the United States of America

The fat grams in this book were obtained from the materials provided by the U.S. Department of Agriculture, the food industry, and computerized data services. This information is assumed to be part of the public domain.

Table of Contents

Dedication   4
Foreword   5
Introduction   6
The Family Dinner Table   13
A Note About The Menus To Mothers   14
Cooking For Life Menus   17

Chapter One	**Appetizers & Snacks** 21	
Chapter Two	**Breakfasts & Beverages** 41	
Chapter Three	**Sweet Breads, Muffins, & Cookies** 61	
Chapter Four	**Soups** 75	
Chapter Five	**Salads** 95	
Chapter Six	**Dressings, Sauces, Spreads, & Dips** 113	
Chapter Seven	**Vegetable Side Dishes** 137	
Chapter Eight	**Grain Side Dishes** 169	
Chapter Nine	**Vegetarian Main Dishes** 197	
Chapter Ten	**Fish** 219	
Chapter Eleven	**Poultry** 231	
Chapter Twelve	**Special Sweet Treats** 249	

Index   265

DEDICATION

Cooking for Life is dedicated to all who desire to eat God's way in order to be strong and healthy to finish the race set before them.

"Write the vision and make it plain on tablets that he may run who reads it."

(Habakkuk 2:2)

"Do you not know that those who run in a race all run, but one receives the prize? Run in such a way that you may obtain it. And everyone who competes for the prize is temperate in all things. Now they do it to obtain a perishable crown. Therefore I run thus; not with uncertainty. Thus I fight: not as one who beats the air. But I discipline my body and bring it into subjection, lest, when I have preached to others, I myself should become disqualified."

(I Corinthians 9:24-27)

FOREWORD

IF YOU ARE **WILLING** AND **OBEDIENT**, YOU SHALL **EAT THE GOOD** OF THE LAND; (ISAIAH 1:19)

The first step to eating God's Way is being **willing** to change your eating habits. You may be overweight, sick, or just plain tired; but, whatever the reason, you have come to a wonderful place in your life! You have come to a crossroads and the sign says, **"I am willing.** " Our wonderful Creator and Father loves you and His Will for your life is to follow His instructions for good health which brings us to the next step.

The second step to eating God's Way is to learn what foods He created for us to eat, learn to prepare them, and begin to eat them. This cookbook is full of delicious recipes made from these wholesome and healthy foods that He created for us and our families. Preparing the foods outlined here insures that you are following or **obeying** God's instructions for good nutrition.

This biblically-based cookbook gives you key nutritional information to **"eat the good of the land."** The wisdom of God and the foods He designed for our bodies were never more needed than at this time. Science and medicine are joining forces to reveal the link between unhealthy eating habits and degenerative diseases. Eating nutritious foods, prepared in a wholesome manner, have now become a matter of life and death. The Lord is a real help in time of need and for this purpose this cookbook is humbly offered.

INTRODUCTION

The study of nutrition predates the science of nutrition by several thousand years. The science of nutrition is in its infancy and therefore nutritional "facts" change from year to year. The changing attitudes, theories, and knowledge about what to eat to be healthy can only be satisfied by returning to the unchanging Word of God. The need for biblically-based nutrition has never been more vital than right now, due to the modern day plagues of heart disease, cancer, diabetes, and obesity.

God is extremely interested in the health of His people. When Israel was delivered out of Egypt, by the hand of a mighty God, one of the fundamental changes He made was in their diet. Our Lord was well aware, even if the children of Israel were not, that food influences the physical, emotional, mental, and spiritual nature of man. But the Lord's emphasis upon the necessity of eating healthy food did not begin in the wilderness of Sinai but in the Garden of Eden.

BACK TO THE GARDEN

Vegetable Kingdom
In the very beginning, in the Book of Genesis, God created man in His Image and according to His Likeness and told man what his diet would be:

"God said, 'See, I have given you (man) every herb (plant) that yields seed which is on the face of the earth, and every tree whose fruit yields seed, to you (man) it shall be for food'."

(Genesis 1:29)

The nutritional program our Creator introduced in the Garden of Eden was a high complex carbohydrate, high fiber, low protein, low fat, low sodium, vegetarian diet. These **"seed-bearing plants"** and the **" trees whose fruit yield seed"** include any food from

INTRODUCTION

the vegetable kingdom that can reproduce itself. These seed-bearing plants are found in the following food groups:

1. Grains, Beans, Legumes
2. Nuts and Seeds
3. Vegetables
4. Fruits

When God changed the diet of the children of Israel, after leaving the slavery of Egypt, He didn't offer them the fatted calf. The Lord's provision for His beloved children was something called, manna. The manna was a seed, like white coriander, and the taste of it was like wafers made with honey (Exodus 16:31). The Israelites made porridge, bread, and pastry cakes out of this seed called Manna and it sustained them very well (Numbers 11:8). God gave the life-sustaining power of seeds, as He had done in the Garden of Eden.

BEYOND THE GARDEN

Animal Kingdom
Red Meats
In addition to God's perfect diet for man, given in Genesis 1:29, our Lord gave us instruction for eating healthy animal foods. In Leviticus 11 and Deuteronomy 14 God tells us to eat animals which have "**divided hoofs and chew their cud.**" These healthy animals are completely vegetarian and are called **herbivores.** Because these animals don't eat the flesh of other animals, they avoid many diseases, as well as worms and parasites carried by other animals. Such healthy herbivores include:

1. Cows   3. Deer   5. Goats
2. Steers 4. Oxen   6. Buffalo

God also identifies animals that are not healthy to eat: the camel, the rock-badger, the hare or rabbit (this class includes all rodents, rats, and squirrels), and the swine (pig or hog) (Leviticus 11:4-7).

Animals that eat both vegetation **and** dead animals are called **omnivores.** Obviously, the indiscriminate eating patterns of **omnivores** (animals that eat both plants and animals), make them potential disease carriers. Pigs for instance, can carry up to 200 diseases and 18 parasites, including the deadly worm called trichinella spiralis commomly called trichinosis. There is no known cure for these spiral worms and they can cripple or even kill anyone that takes even a single forkful of a food that has been contaminated. Pigs also have more incidences of arthritis than any other known animal. In this author's opinion, many diagnosed cases of arthritis will one day be traced to eating arthritic parts of hogs. **I believe that arthritis can be transmitted from pigs to humans through the pig's blood and the eating of its flesh.** A person may be committing slow suicide when they eat ham, bacon, link sausage, or porkchops.

Perhaps many diseases are mis-diagnosed by the medical profession and their real cause is round worm, gullet worms, hook worms, thorn-headed worms, trichina worms, stomach worms, nodular worms, tape worms, as well as many other parasites found in the flesh of the unhealthy swine. Perhaps that's why our Creator told us not to eat them or even touch them (Leviticus 11:8)!

Fish

God declares that only fish that have both **fins and scales** are edible (Leviticus 11:9)! Such fish would include:

1. Bass
2. Cod
3. Flounder
4. Haddock
5. Halibut
6. Perch
7. Red Snapper
8. Salmon
9. Sole
10. Trout
11. Any other fin and scale fish

Not only are the fats (Omega-3 fatty acids) contained in the fin and scale fish able to reduce cholesterol levels in our bodies, but these fish also contain much **lower levels of total fat and calories** than found in red meats.

INTRODUCTION

The inedible fish include some of the world's favorite main courses: shark (no scales), swordfish (no scales), catfish (no scales), shrimp, lobster, crab, clams, scallops, and snails (no fins or scales). These scavenger fish are no less unhealthy than swine, rats or cockroaches, perhaps more so. They contain high levels of cholesterol, mercury, diseases, worms, and parasites. God tells us that these unhealthy fish are an abomination to us not once, but **four times** in three continuous verses:

"...they are an abomination to you. (Levitcus 11:10) ...they shall be an abomination to you ...regard their carcasses as an abomination. (Leviticus 11:11) Whatever in the water does not have fins and scales that shall be an abomination to you." (Leviticus 11:12)

Nowhere else in Scripture does our Lord repeat, four consecutive times such a stern warning. Does the Lord think we are hard of hearing or does He foresee our lustfulness for these "scavengers and rats of the ocean."

Poultry

The remaining passages of Leviticus 11 forbid us to eat the abominable birds such as the eagle, vulture, buzzard, falcon, raven, ostrich, owl, sea gull, hawk, stork, or bat (YUM!); all birds of prey and/or scavengers. These birds eat the flesh of man and beast, taking into their feathery bodies the diseases and parasites of the animals they eat.

So what birds can we eat? The birds that are not birds of prey or scavengers are edible. Such birds as:

1. Quail
2. Duck
3. Chicken
4. Geese
5. Turkey

Eating Dairy Products

There is great controversy in the nutrition community over the eating of dairy products. One side of the debate points to milk and cheese as causing allergies, sinus congestion, mucus build-up, asthma, and constipation. The other side, led by The Dairy Council, claims they are "nature's most perfect foods." We have the history of many healthy cultures around the world (see the book, <u>Lazy Person's Guide to Better Nutrition</u>) who use only small amounts of dairy foods to demonstrate that dairy products are not necessary to get enough calcium or to have optimum health. But what does Scripture say about dairy?

The Lord gave no milk or dairy products to Adam and Eve when He designed the Genesis diet (Genesis 1:29). We also find no reference to milk or dairy products in Leviticus 11 or Deuteronomy 14, when the Lord gave Israel the dietary laws. Israel was not forbidden to eat dairy products, but dairy was not emphasized in God's dietary suggestions, so this cookbook does not emphasize dairy products either.

Perhaps the Lord describes the Promised Land as " flowing with milk and honey" because babies need milk and children like sweets, and the children of Israel were very immature in spiritual matters.

The author's opinion is that milk was intended by God for infants and, although He doesn't forbid us from drinking it, perhaps the reason so many adults are allergic to and bloated from milk is that it is not designed for adults. Milk should be taken sparingly and curdled milk products like yogurt and kefir are preferred because of easier digestion than straight milk or cheese. Any recipes in this cookbook using lowfat and nonfat dairy products, or any ingredients for that matter, can be changed or removed at reader's discretion.

INTRODUCTION

Eating Animal Fats

The American Cancer Society and the National Cancer Institute spend millions of dollars to warn Americans of the dangers of eating too much animal fat. The American Heart Association warns us that eating too much saturated animal fat, high in cholesterol, is a major cause of heart disease and strokes. Saturated animal fat, according to the American Cancer Society, is also prime culprit in certain types of cancer. The animal fat eaten in great abundance (40% of total calories), throughout America, is also responsible for obesity problems in two out of every five people. It is vitally important that all of us cut down on fat, especially animal fat. God's Word is found to be true again.

> *"This shall be a perpetual statute throughout your generations in all your dwellings; you shall eat neither fat nor blood."*
> *(Leviticus 3:17)*

> *"You shall not eat any fat, of ox or sheep or goat."*
> *(Leviticus 7:23)*

There are many references in the Scriptures from God to man not to eat animal fat, but there is a purpose for animal fat, offer it to Him!

> *"....and the priest shall burn them on the altar as food, an offering made by fire for a sweet aroma; all the fat is the Lord's."*
> *(Leviticus 3:16)*

The burning of animal fat is " a sweet aroma" for anyone who has smelled a sizzling steak cooked over mesquite wood, or barbecued steak on a portable grill, or fried chicken, or the aroma as you pass a fast food hamburger restaurant.

CONCLUSION

This cookbook will help you cut back on the high fat, high cholesterol foods that prematurely take our precious lives, and teach you how to prepare the healthy foods of God that can help maintain or regain health. After all, who knows better what foods we should put in our bodies than He who created our bodies?

The health of this generation is not dependent upon scientists, doctors, or hospitals. Our health and the health of our children rest in the hands of the Lord. His Word is as clear about nutrition as it is on every aspect of our lives. If the future of America depends upon the survival of the family, then the cooks of households throughout America must learn to cook God's foods to preserve the family. To help the family **endure** in these final days is the prayer and purpose of this cookbook.

The Family Dinner Table

Recent studies suggest that fifty percent of all the food dollars in American families are spent outside the home. This statistic is another reason that the American Family is in trouble. With the family members going in so many different directions, the fast food restaurants have become an easy solution to a fast paced lifestyle.

Unfortunately for the family unit, eating outside the home does not foster closeness, togetherness, or understanding. All day long family members have been going their separate ways, and it is vital to the spiritual, as well as the physical health of the family, that they gather for the evening meal (during the busy week). The weekends should be a time of even more meals eaten <u>AS A FAMILY.</u> We must be diligent to bring back the family dinners around the dinner table.

At family meals, the individual members can look around the table to see they are part of a team. They can also share what happens at school, at the office, or any other important or unimportant information. **Eating together as a family in the privacy and quiet of your own home is not a luxury, it's a necessity.** Eating nutritious home-cooked meals with other family members is quality time in a relaxed atmosphere.

In order to accomplish the restoration of family dining at home, wives must be willing to find time to prepare nutritious, lowfat meals that will help sustain the health of their husband and their children. Mothers are the "nutritional chefs" of their family and are therefore responsible to work towards home-cooked meals that build intimacy and security for their families.

<u>Cooking For Life</u> , I trust will help wives and mothers to accomplish this transition back to the Family dinner table.

Gordon S. Tessler
Dr. Gordon S. Tessler

A Note About the Menus to Mothers

When planning the menus we tried to include combinations of meals that were easy to prepare, along with those that would take a little more time. However, for those mothers with active children, who seem to always be on the go, here are some tips for integrating The Genesis Way into your busy lifestyle.

1. Plan ahead! This could save you hours and lots of anxiety! Use the menus we have prepared or plan your own. See if there are any preparations you can do ahead, for instance, soaking beans, preparing a marinade, chopping fruits and vegetables, etc.

2. Post your menus on the refrigerator. Everyone knows what to expect and this tends to reduce stress and complaints.

3. Involve your child/children in setting the table, cooking and cleaning up after meals. The rule at our house is that each person must rinse their dishes after <u>each</u> meal and put them in the dishwasher.

4. During the school year, mornings can be pretty hectic around the Tessler household. We need breakfasts that are quick and filling. Because we believe in the importance of grains in the diet, we have established Monday, Wednesday and Friday mornings as oatmeal days.

This makes a quick healthy breakfast that will get your child/children off to the right start. We use old-fashioned rolled oats and prepare them according to the directions on the box. Add a little cinnamon, raisins, honey, and skim milk. Toasted bagels with all-fruit spread and fresh fruit can also be a time saver on those hectic mornings. On the weekends we splurge and make special breakfasts that take a little more time to prepare. Weekends are a good time to make a double batch of muffins, pancakes, etc. to be used later in the week.

5. Most children do not want to appear different than their peers and this also applies to what they carry to school for lunch. Our children prefer to take a sandwich made with whole grain bread, some kind of lowfat chips and cookies, and fruit for snack. Their sandwich selections include: a slice of turkey breast with lettuce and tomato, natural peanut butter or almond butter with either sliced bananas or all-fruit jam, or a pita sandwich stuffed with salad and a little turkey breast. Sometimes, when I have made black bean burritos, quesadilles, or homemade pizza for dinner, they will take those for lunch the next day. Occasionally, they will take leftover soup and salad from the night before. No-sugar added lowfat yogurt cups are also good for bag lunches. To drink, we send all-fruit juice boxes such as Juicy Juice or Minute Maid 100% Apple Juice. Better yet, buy the small containers of distilled water and send those to school. Water is actually the perfect thirst quencher.

6. We believe in serving one another and with three children we have applied this principle to making school lunches. Each child takes a week and it is his or her responsibility to get up, find out what each child wants, and fix the school lunches each day that week. This has worked very well in our house!

7. Each month we allow our children to buy two (2) school lunches and two (2) snacks. They have the freedom to choose which lunches and what snacks they want. This way we know that they are getting healthy lunches the rest of the month even if they decide to splurge.

8. Use an automatic, non-stick grain/rice cooker. It makes life The Genesis Way very simple and convenient. Your grains cook in about half the time and turn off automatically. You can even put a timer on the unit so it will turn on and off to fit your busy schedule.

As you go through the program, we're sure you will come up with your own time-saving ideas and recipes. Please share them with us by writing or calling. We'd love to hear from you.

Eat Well,

Laura A. Tessler

Laura Tessler

WEEK 1

DAY	BREAKFAST	LUNCH	DINNER
Sunday	Breakfast Bars with Orange Wedges Juice or Hot Tea	Salmon Pattie On Whole Grain Bun w/ Lettuce & Tamato Marinated Fruit Salad	Laura's Lentil Stew Mixed Green Salad w/tbsp.non-fat dressing Fat Free Crackers
Monday	Spiced Breakfast Millet Juice or Hot Tea	Veggie Pita Pocket Fresh Fruit Almond Raspberry Torte	Quinoa Chicken Sauteed Zucchini & Carrots Gingerbread
Tuesday	3 Banana Pancakes w/ Fresh Banana Slices & Maple Syrup Juice or Hot Tea	Black Bean Burritos Fruit Kabob	Italian Veg. Pie Tomato Millet Casserole Whole Grain Bread
Wednesday	Outstanding Oats Cantaloupe Wedge Hot Tea	Potato-Leek Soup Mixed Green Salad Fat Free Crackers	Lemon Basil Chicken Tenders Vegetable Medley Brown Rice Pilaf
Thursday	Mexican Omelet Half a Grapefruit Whole Grain Toast Juice or Hot Tea	Southwest Marinated Bean Salad Fat Free Tortilla Chips	Rice Stuffed Eggplant Sweet Carrots Green Beans w/ Pimento Strip
Friday	Bagel with All Fruit Spread Apple Slices Juice or Hot Tea	Baked Potato w/ Barley Vegetable Chili Steamed Broccoli 2 Oatmeal-Raisin Cookies	Vegetable Lasagna Tomato-Cucumber Salad Whole Wheat Roll
Saturday	Whole Wheat Waffles w/ Pure Maple Syrup or Pourable Fruit Spread Fresh Strawberries	Tomato Basil Couscous Salad w/ Herbed Pita Chips	Grilled Garlic-Basil Grouper Grilled Vegetables Lemon-Dill Rice

WEEK 2

DAY	BREAKFAST	LUNCH	DINNER
Sunday	Millet Fruit Pudding Bowl of Fresh Strawberries & Kiwi	Roast Turkey Breast Green Bean Bundle Gala Garlic Potato Mash Lemon Biscuits	Grain Burgers w/ Tomato & Lettuce Sweet Slaw Carrot Cake
Monday	2-3 Oatmeal Snack Cakes Grapefruit Half	Pita Stuffed w/ Lettuce, Tomato, & Turkey Small Bunch of Grapes Carrot Cake	Black Bean Soup over Rice Sunshine Spinach Salad
Tuesday	Bagel w/ Apple Butter Banana Juice or Hot Tea	Black Bean Soup Orange Cabbage Carrot Salad Fat Free Crackers	Honey Mustard Chicken Sweet Brown & Wild Rice with Sugar Snaps & Sweet Peppers
Wednesday	Oatmeal w/ Cinnamon & Raisins Juice or Hot Tea	Chef Salad w/ Turkey Breast Assorted Fresh Vegetables 1 tbsp. Vinaigrette Fat Free Crackers	Spinach-Basil Pasta Mixed Green Salad Apple Pie Dessert Topping over Frozen Yogurt
Thursday	2 Best Ever Bran Muffins Apple Slices Juice or Tea	Rio Grande Quinoa & Corn in Crispy Tortilla bowl Carrot Sticks	Turkey Chili Millet Stuffed Squash
Friday	Orange Pancakes w/ Orange Syrup Juice or Hot Tea	Vegetable Pasta Salad Pita Bread Fresh Pear	Lemon Dill Fish Colorful Stuffed Peppers Carrot Raisin Salad Sweet Corn Muffin
Saturday	Weekend Breakfast Quiche Grapefruit half Juice or Hot Tea	Vegetable Barley Soup Fat Free Crackers Crispy Rice Bars	Family Favorite Lowfat Pizza Tossed Salad

WEEK 3

BREAKFAST	LUNCH	DINNER	DAY
Applesauce Muffins w/ Cinnamon Applesauce Juice or Hot Tea	Pepper Chicken and Rice Fresh Fruit Salad	Nine Bean Soup Steamed Cauliflower, Carrots, & Broccoli w/ Herb Sauce Apple Sauce Muffin	Sunday
Oatmeal Snack Cakes Fresh Melon Balls Juice or Hot Tea	Baked Potato w/ Nine Bean Soup & Steamed Broccoli	Chicken Fajita Pita Pocket	Monday
Bagels w/ All Fruit Spread Banana/Strawberry Yogurt Juice or Hot Tea	Colorful Brown Rice Salad Herbed Pita Chips Oatmeal Banana Cookie	Marinara Sauce over Millet Supreme Whole Wheat Bread Mixed Green Salad w/ tbsp. Lowfat Italian Dressing	Tuesday
Outstanding Oats Fresh Pear & Kiwi Juice or Hot Tea	Mexican Pizza Fresh Vegetable Dip w/ Carrot Strips & Broccoli, etc.	Barley-Bulgur Veg. Casserole Sweet Sauteed Sugar Snaps	Wednesday
Strawberry Pancakes w/ Strawberry Pourable Fruit Fresh Strawberries Juice or Hot Tea	Crunchy Barley Salad Fresh Fruit Salad Herbed Pita Chips	Pasta Faggioli Mixed Green Salad w/ Vinaigrette	Thursday
Spiced Breakfast Millet Juice or Hot Tea	White Beans w/ Sage Sauteed Spinach & Garlic	Orange Orange Roughy Elegant Eggplant Provencal Apple Sweet Potatos	Friday
Whole Wheat Waffles w/ Pure Maple Syrup Half a Grapefruit	Black Bean Burrito Spinach Dip & Fresh Vegetables	Stuffed Turkey Tenderloins Zucchini Fans Orange Herb Rice Mandarin Orange Cake	Saturday

WEEK 4

BREAKFAST	LUNCH	DINNER	DAY
Chewy Apple Oat Bars Apple Slices Juice or Hot Tea	Pasta Madelena Mixed Green Salad Whole Grain Roll	Broccoli Bisque Fat Free Crackers Apple Acorn Squash	Sunday
Orange Muffins Fresh Orange Slices Juice or Hot Tea	Black Bean & Barley Salad Steamed Garlic Broccoli Bagel Chips	Chicken & Pepper Stir-Fry w/ Almonds over Brown Rice Orange Muffin	Monday
Oatmeal w/ Raisins & Cinnamon Juice or Hot Tea	Luscious Lentil Soup Salad w/ Mixed Greens & Vegtables Fat Free Crackers	Eggplant Couscous Rolls Squash & Onions Whole Grain Roll	Tuesday
Millet Fruit Pudding w/ Fresh Strawberries Half a Bagel Juice or Hot Tea	Chickpea Sandwich Spread in Pita Pocket w/ Tomato Cucumbers, Lettuce, & Sprouts Carrot Sticks	Grain Roast Zucchini Tomato Bake Spiked Carrots & Onions	Wednesday
Mexican Omelet Whole Grain Toast Juice or Hot Tea	Pita Pizza Mixed Green Salad w/ Basil Vinaigrette Dressing	Orange Basil Chicken Mandarin Orange Millet Sauteed Spinach & Garlic	Thursday
Cranberry Muffins w/ Orange & Grapefruit Sections	Veggie Pita Pocket w/ A Slice of Turkey or Chicken Breast Seasonal Fruit	Cabbage Soup Quinoa & Squash Casserole Cranberry Muffins	Friday
Weekend Breakfast Quiche Grapefruit Half Juice or Hot Tea	Cabbage Soup Mixed Green Salad Pita w/ Chickpea Sandwich Spread	Dilled Salmon Carrot-Rice Casserole Dilled Asparagus Cranberry Muffin	Saturday

CHAPTER ONE

Appetizers & Snacks

"And their father Israel said to them, ' If it must be so, then do this: Take some of the best fruits of the land in your vessels and carry down a present for the man-a little balm and a little honey, spices and myrrh, pistachio nuts and almonds.'"

(Genesis 43:11)

APPETIZERS & SNACKS

NUTS AND SEEDS

We suggest you eat the good fats contained in the cholesterol-free nuts and seeds. Just a few nuts or seeds make a great snack. They are also rich in high quality protein, vitamins and minerals. They should be considered as an excellent alternative to animal protein and are economical since only a handful are necessary. Nuts and seeds are extremely versatile, providing delicious variety in the diet. They store well, especially in the freezer or refrigerator and they travel well. When you purchase nuts and seeds, make certain they are not roasted, toasted, boiled, or cooked in any way. Eating only raw nuts and seeds insures you that the fats, protein, vitamins and minerals have not been damaged by excess heat. They should be salt-free too. Nuts can be purchased in or out of the shell. Some examples of healthful nuts include almonds*, Brazil nuts, cashews, filberts, pecans, and walnuts. Peanuts are not nuts! They are a member of the legume family. Some examples of healthful seeds include flax, pumpkin, sesame, and sunflower.

> The ancient tradition of giving nuts as offerings of peace and goodwill has been carried down through the centuries. In areas of the present day Holy Land, Kibbet (Hebrew for "treat") is served to visitors along with dates, figs and raisins.

Almonds are the Best
* All nuts are high in complete protein, cholesterol-free fatty acids, fiber, vitamins and minerals yet the almond is considered "King of the nuts." They have generous amounts of calcium, magnesium, potassium, iron, B-vitamins, vitamin C, and protein, making them an almost perfect food. According to the Scriptures, almonds were given as gifts to kings (Genesis 43:11). Almond blossoms were also God's choice for the design of the bowls and lamp stand in the Tabernacle and later in the Temple (Exodus 25:34-35). The "miracle rod" of Aaron that blossomed and was placed in the Ark of the Covenant, was none other than the branch of an almond tree (Numbers 17:8-10 . Hebrews 9:4).

Ants on a Log
(Better known as: "Celery with Peanut Butter and Raisins")

2 stalks of celery
2-4 tablespoons natural peanut butter
   (or almond butter)
Raisins

Cut celery into 4 equal parts.
Fill center cavity with peanut butter and place raisins on top. (See - it looks like ants on a log!)
Yield: 4 servings

*Although high in fat, this makes a great mid-morning or afterschool snack for children not watching their weight.

Per Serving:
Calories: 77
Fat: 4 grams
Carbohydrate: 10 grams
Protein: 2 grams
Cholesterol: 0 milligrams
Sodium: 20 milligrams
Dietary Fiber: 1 gram

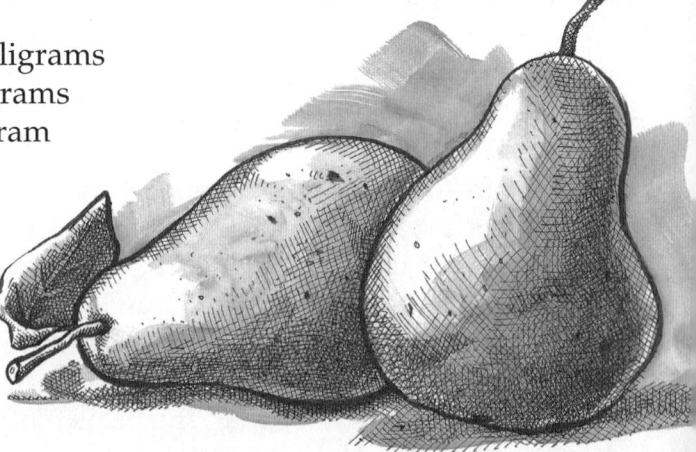

Appetizing Chicken Wontons
(These make great appetizers for parties.)

2 boneless, skinless chicken breast halves, cut into 1/4-inch strips
1 clove garlic, minced
1/2 cup shredded carrot
1/4 cup finely chopped celery
1 tablespoon low-sodium soy sauce
1 tablespoon dry sherry
1 tablespoon fresh lime juice
1/2-1 teaspoon ground ginger
2 teaspoons cornstarch
32 wonton wrappers (about half a package)
Vegetable cooking spray

Process chicken in food processor until ground, about 1 minute.

Cook chicken and garlic in a nonstick skillet until chicken is no longer pink. Drain.

Combine chicken and garlic with next 7 ingredients; mixing well.

Spoon 1 teaspoon into center of each wonton wrapper; moisten edges with water. Carefully bring 2 opposite points of wrapper to center over filling; pinch points together. Bring 2 remaining opposite points to center, and pinch together.

Place wonton on baking sheet that has been lightly sprayed with cooking spray. Spray each wonton lightly with cooking spray.

Bake at 375 degrees for 8-10 minutes until lightly browned.

Yield: 2 1/2 dozen

Per Serving:
Calories: 20
Fat: 1 gram
Carbohydrate: 1 gram
Protein: 2 grams
Cholesterol: 10 milligrams
Sodium: 30 milligrams
Dietary Fiber: 0 grams

Bagel Chips

2 whole wheat bagels
Olive oil vegetable cooking spray
Dried oregano

Slice bagels very thin into rounds.
Lightly spray each bagel round with vegetable cooking spray.
Sprinkle with oregano.
Bake at 375 degrees for 10-12 minutes until crisp and golden.
Yield: 2-3 servings

Per Serving:
Calories: 176
Fat: 0 grams
Carbohydrate: 37 grams
Protein: 7 grams
Cholesterol: 0 milligrams
Sodium: 345 milligrams
Dietary Fiber: 0 grams

Banana Boats

(This makes a great afterschool snack or anytime fun treat.)

1 medium to large banana
2 tablespoons strawberry-banana nonfat yogurt
   (or any other fruit flavor)
2 raw almonds, chopped

Carefully slit the top of banana peel lengthwise, leaving about 1-inch uncut at each end.

Cut away about 1/2-inch of the peel on each side of the slit with scissors.

Scoop out banana in small pieces with a teaspoon and put in bowl.

Add 2 tablespoons yogurt to banana and stir, mashing some of the banana.

Fill the banana peel with yogurt mixture and sprinkle chopped almonds on top. (You may want to put a fresh pitted cherry on top. Use your imagination! The possibilities are endless - almost).

Yield: 1 serving

Per Serving:
Calories: 159
Fat: 3 grams
Carbohydrate: 30 grams
Protein: 4 grams
Cholesterol: 0 milligrams
Sodium: 18 milligrams
Dietary Fiber: 4 grams

Banana-Yogurt Popsicles

2 ripe bananas
2 ounces plain nonfat yogurt
1/4 cup apple juice concentrate

Break the bananas into chunks and place into small bowls. Mash thoroughly.
Add next 2 ingredients and blend well.
Pour into popsicle molds. Freeze until hard.
Yield: 6 servings

Per Serving:
Calories: 59
Fat: 0 grams
Carbohydrate: 14 grams
Protein: 1 gram
Sodium: 9 milligrams
Dietary Fiber: 1 gram

Crispy Tortilla Bowls
(These fat-free flour tortillas also make great crackers!*)

6 Fat Free flour tortillas
Vegetable Cooking Spray
6 (8 ounce) Pyrex custard cups

Spray each custard cup lightly with vegetable cooking spray.

Place tortillas in microwave oven and heat on HI for 20-30 seconds. (This will make the tortillas pliable and easier to work with). If you prefer not to use a microwave, slightly dampen each tortilla by brushing with a basting brush that has been dipped in warm water.

Place one tortilla in each Pyrex dish arranging it so that each tortilla forms the shape of a bowl. (The top of the tortilla will naturally curve making a interesting shaped bowl).

Bake at 300 degrees for 10-15 minutes or until lightly browned around the top edges. Remove from Pyrex dishes and cool. (You want your tortilla bowls to be crisp).

Serve with any of the grain salads or marinated fresh fruit salads.

Yield: 6 servings

*Note: To make fat-free crackers, place tortillas on a non-stick baking sheet and bake at 350 degrees for 7-10 minutes. When lightly browned, turn over and bake until lightly browned on other side. Allow to cool and break into cracker-like pieces.

Per Serving:
Calories: 110
Fat: 0 grams
Carbohydrate: 24 grams
Protein: 2 grams
Cholesterol: 0 milligrams
Sodium: 140 milligrams
Dietary Fiber: 1 gram

Corn Tortilla Chips

4 corn tortillas
Olive Oil vegetable cooking spray

Cut corn tortillas in 8 wedges each.
Bake at 400 degrees for 8-10 minutes, or until crisp and golden.
Serve with Garlic Bean Dip or Spinach Dip
Yield: 4 servings

Per Serving:
Calories: 56
Fat: 1 gram
Carbohydrate: 12 grams
Protein: 0 grams
Cholesterol: 0 milligrams
Sodium: 3 milligrams
Dietary Fiber: 1 gram

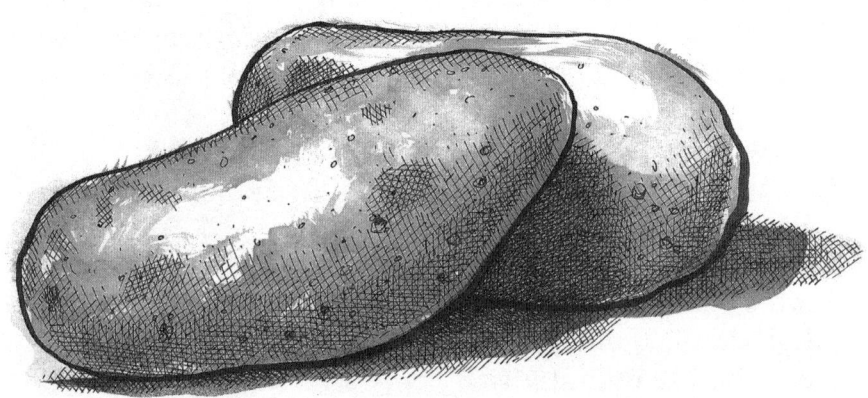

Crispy Rice Bars

These are a good alternative to the traditional rice crispy treats made with marshmallows. They're just as sweet and crunchy and kids love them.

2 teaspoons olive oil
1/2 cup brown rice syrup
1/2 teaspoon almond extract
4 cups crispy brown rice cereal
Vegetable cooking spray

Combine olive oil, brown rice syrup, and almond extract in large saucepan and heat over low heat until warm and runny.
Stir in rice cereal and coat well.
Spoon into 8x8x2 glass dish that has been sprayed with vegetable cooking spray.
Place in refrigerator to firm-up and then cut into squares. (Storing them in the refrigerator will keep them firm and crispy).
Yield: 1 dozen

Per Bar:
Calories: 146
Fat: 1 gram
Carbohydrate: 32 grams
Protein: 2 grams
Cholesterol: 0 milligrams
Sodium: 341 milligrams
Dietary Fiber: 0 grams

Date-Filled Wonton Tarts

12 wonton wrappers
1 cup pitted dates, chopped
6 tablespoons fresh orange juice
4 tablespoons chopped pecans
1 tablespoon grated orange rind
Vegetable cooking spray

Press wonton wrappers into the cups of a minimuffin pan to form shells.
Spray each shell lightly with vegetable cooking spray.
Bake at 350 degrees for 5 minutes, or until golden brown.
While wrappers are baking, combine dates and orange juice in a small saucepan and cook over medium heat 3 to 4 minutes until orange juice is absorbed.
Add pecan pieces and rind.
Fill each wonton shell with 1 tablespoon of date mixture and serve.
Yield: 1 dozen

Per Tart:
Calories: 75
Fat: 1 gram
Carbohydrate: 17 grams
Protein: 1 gram
Cholesterol: 1 milligram
Sodium: 46 milligrams
Dietary Fiber: 1 gram

APPETIZERS & SNACKS

Fruitsicles

1 cup apple juice, no sugar added
1 cup of fresh or frozen fruit (such as strawberries, peaches, pineapple, or raspberries)
Sprinkle of lemon juice

Place apple juice and fruit in blender. Puree until smooth.
Pour into popsicle molds and freeze.
Yield: 6 servings

Per Serving:
Calories: 62
Fat: 0 grams
Carbohydrate: 16 grams
Protein: 0 grams
Cholesterol: 0 milligrams
Sodium: 2 milligrams
Dietary Fiber: 2 grams

Fruit Kabobs

8 fresh pineapple chunks
8 fresh orange sections
4 kiwi slices, halved(1/2-inch thick)
8 fresh whole strawberries
Wooden Skewers

    Beginning with pineapple chunks, alternate fruit on wooden skewers to make a colorful and delicious snack or accompaniment for any meal.
    Serve with Orange-Yogurt Dip (see recipe)
    Yield: 4 servings

*You may want to add other fresh fruit that is in season such as: watermelon, cantaloupe, and honeydew.

Per Serving:
Calories: 72
Fat: 0 grams
Carbohydrate: 18 grams
Protein: 1 gram
Cholesterol: 0 milligrams
Sodium: 4 milligrams
Dietary Fiber: 4 grams

Herbed Pita Chips

2 whole wheat pita pockets,
   (fat-free)
2 teaspoons Parmesan cheese
Dried oregano and basil
Olive oil vegetable cooking spray, (such as Pam)

Divide a whole pita pocket in half. Lightly spray with cooking spray and sprinkle with grated Parmesan cheese, dried oregano and basil.

Cut each half into 6 wedges and bake at 400 degrees for 8-10 minutes, or until crisp and golden.

Yield: 3 servings

Per Serving:
Calories: 105
Fat: 0 grams
Carbohydrate: 23 grams
Protein: 5 grams
Cholesterol: 0 milligrams
Sodium: 234 milligrams
Dietary Fiber: 3 grams

Millet Spinach Appetizers

2 (10 ounce) packages chopped spinach,
    thawed and squeezed
1 cup cooked millet
1/3 cup Parmesan cheese
2 tablespoons butter
1/4 cup egg beaters
3/4 teaspoon garlic salt
Vegetable cooking spray

Combine all ingredients except cooking spray in a large mixing bowl. Blend well.

Shape into small cocktail-sized balls.

Place balls on a baking sheet that has been sprayed lightly with cooking spray.

Bake at 350 degrees for 15-20 minutes or until the balls are browned on the bottom.

Yield: 6 servings

*For a more festive look, stick a colored toothpick into each spinach ball and serve. You can also make these into bars or triangle shapes by cooking them in either an 8x8 baking dish or a glass pie pan.

Per Serving:
Calories: 138
Fat: 6 grams
Carbohydrate: 15 grams
Protein: 8 grams
Cholesterol: 14 milligrams
Sodium: 513 milligrams
Dietary Fiber: 3 grams

Orange-Yogurt Popsicles

1 (6-ounce) can frozen orange juice, thawed
6 ounces water
1 cup plain nonfat yogurt
1 teaspoon vanilla
1 tablespoon honey or brown rice syrup

Combine all ingredients together in blender and blend.
Pour into popsicle molds and freeze.
Yield: 6 servings

Per Serving:
Calories: 85
Fat: 0 grams
Carbohydrate: 19 grams
Protein: 3 grams
Cholesterol: 1 milligram
Sodium: 27 milligrams
Dietary Fiber: 0 grams

Raggedy Anne Salad

1 lettuce leaf
1 peach half
1 slice cucumber
4 thin celery sticks
Raisins
1/4 carrot, shredded or grated

Place lettuce on a plate. Place peach half in the center of the lettuce leaf to serve as Raggedy Anne's body. Use the cucumber slice for the head.

Arrange the celery sticks as legs and arms. Decorate the head and body with raisins for eyes, nose, mouth, and buttons. Use the shredded carrot for hair.

Eat and enjoy!

Yield: 1 serving

Per Serving:
Calories: 44
Fat: 0 grams
Carbohydrate: 11 grams
Protein: 1 gram
Cholesterol: 0 milligrams
Sodium: 41 milligrams
Dietary Fiber: 2 grams

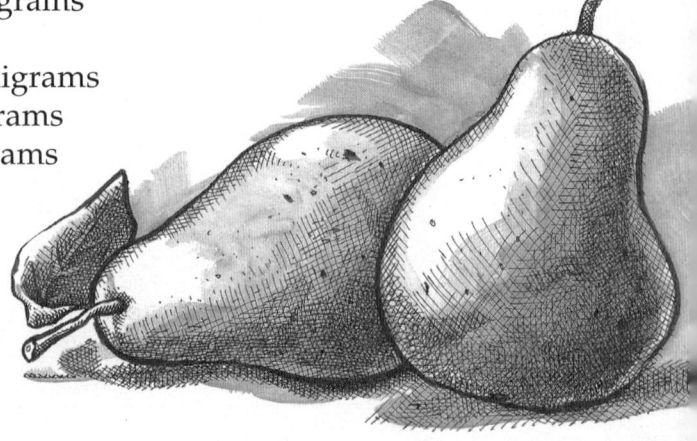

APPETIZERS & SNACKS

Strawberry Sorbet Pops

1/4 cup water
4 tablespoons brown rice syrup or honey
1/2 fresh lemon
1 tablespoon orange juice
2 cups fresh strawberries, frozen may be used

Combine first 4 ingredients in small saucepan and bring to a boil. Remove from heat and pour mixture into blender with the strawberries.
Blend until smooth. Pour into popsicle molds and freeze. (If you prefer, you can freeze sorbet in a large plastic bowl and scoop into dessert dishes to serve).
Yield: 6 servings

Per Serving:
Calories: 63
Fat: 0 grams
Carbohydrate: 17 grams
Protein: 0 grams
Cholesterol: 0 milligrams
Sodium: 3 milligrams
Dietary Fiber: 1 gram

Suckers

1/2 teaspoon canola oil
3/4 cup brown rice syrup
1 teaspoon flavoring (i.e.,Lemon, Orange, Raspberry extract)

Pour oil into heavy saucepan. Heat slightly over medium heat.
Add syrup and flavoring. Cook until bubbly. Reduce heat and stir 5 minutes or until a drop of syrup in water forms hard ball (hard ball stage).
Remove from heat and cool just until mixture is able to be handled. Spray fingers with vegetable cooking spray and form into balls. Insert stick or put stick on wax paper and pour syrup over. Wrap in plastic wrap when cooled and store in refrigerator.
Yield: 12 suckers

Per Serving:
Calories: 42
Fat: 0 grams
Carbohydrate: 10 grams
Protein: 0 grams
Cholesterol: 0 milligrams
Sodium: 0 milligrams
Dietary Fiber: 0 grams

CHAPTER TWO

Breakfasts & Beverages

"a land of wheat and barley, of vines and fig trees and pomegranates, a land of olive oil and honey;"

(Deuteronomy 8:8)

Almond Milk

1/2 cup raw almonds
1 tablespoon maple syrup (optional)
2 cups water

Place almonds in blender and grind to a fine powder.
Add maple syrup, if desired, and 1 cup of water. Blend for 1-2 minutes.
While blender is running at high speed, pour remaining cup of water through opening in blender lid. Blend 2 minutes.
Place a strainer over a large bowl. Line strainer with cheesecloth or a paper coffee filter.
Pour almond milk slowly into strainer.
Yield: 2 cups

Per 1 Cup Serving:
Calories: 235
Fat: 19 grams
Carbohydrate: 14 grams
Protein: 7 grams
Cholesterol: 0 milligrams
Sodium: 5 milligrams
Dietary Fiber: 4 grams

Banana Milkshake
(Children of all ages will love this shake!)

1 cup Almond Milk (see recipe)
2 frozen bananas medium sized

Combine both ingredients in a blender. Blend until smooth and serve.
Yield: 2 servings

Variation: Add either 1 large peach or 6 large fresh strawberries to above ingredients for a Peach or Strawberry Milkshake.

Per Serving:
Calories: 340
Fat: 20 grams
Carbohydrate: 41 grams
Protein: 8 grams
Cholesterol: 0 milligrams
Sodium: 6 milligrams
Dietary Fiber: 7 grams

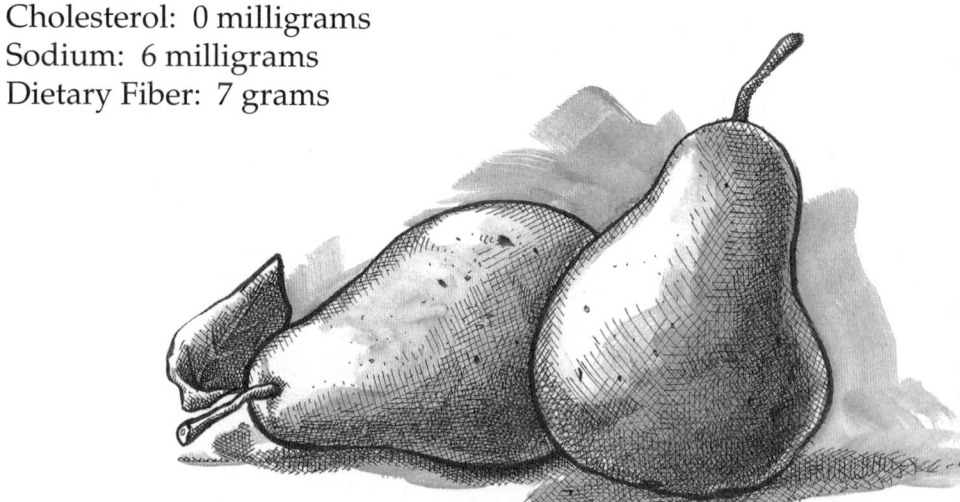

Banana Pancakes

1 cup whole wheat flour
2 teaspoons baking powder,
   Rumford aluminum-free
1 1/4 cup nonfat buttermilk

2 tablespoons unsweetened
   applesauce
1 medium-sized ripe banana,
   finely chopped

Mix flour and baking powder together.
Mix buttermilk and applesauce together. Add to flour and stir just until flour is moistened.
Fold in banana.
Spoon batter onto a nonstick griddle and cook.
Yield: 12 pancakes

Per Pancake:
Calories: 54
Fat: 0 grams
Carbohydrate: 11 grams
Protein: 2 grams
Cholesterol: 1 milligram
Sodium: 88 milligrams
Dietary Fiber: 1 grams

Banana Smoothie

2 cups plain nonfat yogurt
2 medium bananas, (that have been peeled and frozen)
1/2 cup apple juice
1/2 cup strawberries, fresh or frozen
6 ice cubes

Combine all ingredients except for the ice in a blender. Blend until smooth.
Add ice and blend again. Serve in chilled glasses.
Yield: 3-4 servings

*__Variation:__ Omit yogurt and apple juice and substitute 1 cup crushed pineapple and 1/2 cup apple juice concentrate.

Per Serving:
Calories: 128
Fat: 0 grams
Carbohydrate: 26 grams
Protein: 7 grams
Cholesterol: 3 milligrams
Sodium: 72 milligrams
Dietary Fiber: 2 grams

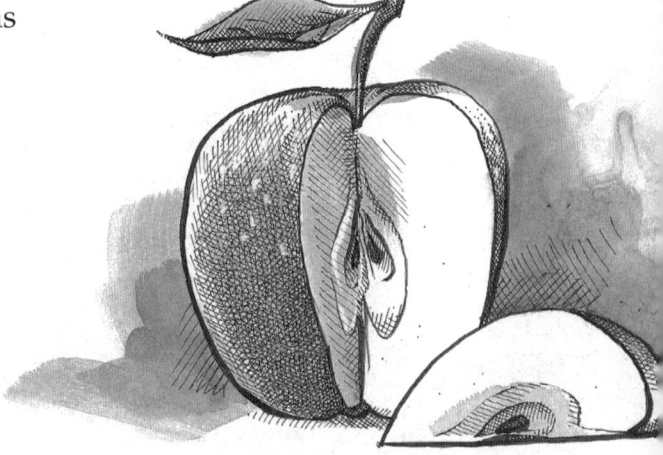

Breakfast Bars

1 1/2 cups rolled oats, uncooked
3/4 cup chopped dates
1/2 teaspoon grated orange rind
1 teaspoon cinnamon
1/2 teaspoon sea salt
1/4 cup chopped pecans

1/4 cup water
1/2 cup unsweetened applesauce
1/4 cup nonfat plain yogurt
1 shredded medium apple
Vegetable cooking spray

Combine all ingredients in a large bowl and mix well. Let stand at room temperature for 10 minutes.

Press mixture into an 8" x 8" baking dish that has been lightly sprayed with vegetable cooking spray.

Bake at 375 degrees for 20-25 minutes. Cool slightly and cut into 6 bars.

Yield: 6 servings

Per Bar:
Calories: 196
Fat: 5 grams
Carbohydrate: 37 grams
Protein: 5 grams
Cholesterol: 0 milligrams
Sodium: 202 milligrams
Dietary Fiber: 5 grams

Holiday "Eggnog"

(Serve this deliciously, rich, and creamy drink as a holiday treat! It may not be low in fat but it does contain the essential fatty acids that the body needs with no added cholesterol).

2 cups Almond Milk
2 medium-sized fresh bananas
1/4 teaspoon grated nutmeg
1/2 teaspoon vanilla
Dash of nutmeg

Combine all ingredients in blender. Blend until smooth.
Serve in glasses with a dash of nutmeg on top. (Be sure to serve immediately after making).
Yield: 4 servings

Per Serving:
Calories: 173
Fat: 10 grams
Carbohydrate: 21 grams
Protein: 4 grams
Cholesterol: 0 milligrams
Sodium: 3 milligrams
Dietary Fiber: 3 grams

Hot Apple Punch

2 (12-ounce) cans frozen unsweetened apple juice concentrate
   thawed and undiluted
1 quart water
2 cups fresh cranberries
2 sticks cinnamon
6 whole cloves

Prepare apple juice according to the directions on the can.
Pour into a large Dutch oven and add remaining ingredients.
Bring to a boil and cover, reduce heat, and simmer for 30 minutes.
Strain mixture, removing cranberries and spices. Serve.
Yield: 1 gallon

Per 1 Cup Serving:
Calories: 50
Fat: 0 grams
Carbohydrate: 12 grams
Protein: 0 grams
Cholesterol: 0 milligrams
Sodium: 7 milligrams
Dietary Fiber: 0 grams

Holiday Wassail

2 quarts apple cider or juice
1 pint cranberry juice
1/2 - 1 teaspoon allspice
1 stick cinnamon
1 orange studded with whole cloves (about 7)

Mix all ingredients in crock pot. Cover and cook on high for 1 hour then on low for 3-4 hours. (*Options: Cook in crock pot on low for 6-8 hours or cook on stovetop in Dutch oven on low for 3 hours)
Yield: 10 cups

Per Serving:
Calories: 129
Fat: 0 grams
Carbohydrate: 33 grams
Protein: 0 grams
Cholesterol: 0 milligrams
Sodium: 7 milligrams
Dietary Fiber: 1 gram

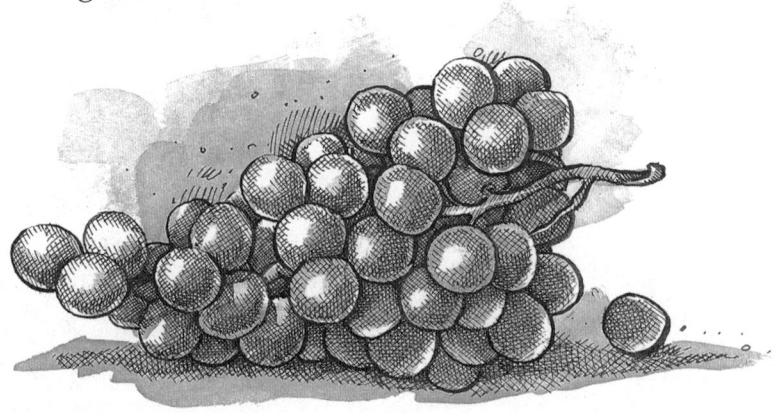

Oatmeal Snack Cakes

1 1/2 cups old-fashioned
  rolled oats, uncooked
1 teaspoon cinnamon
1/2 cup raisins
1/2 cup chopped dates
1/2 cup unsweetened crushed
  pineapple, undrained
1 large apple; peeled, cored,
  and chopped
1 egg white
1 1/2 teaspoons Rumford
  aluminum-free
  baking powder
1 teaspoon vanilla
Vegetable cooking spray

Combine first 4 ingredients in large mixing bowl; mix well. Set aside.

Combine remaining ingredients except cooking spray in blender and process until smooth.

Add pineapple mixture to dry ingredients and stir until well blended.

Spoon mixture evenly into muffin pan that has been lightly sprayed with cooking spray.

Bake at 350 degrees for 35 minutes. (These cakes will not rise during baking).

Yield: 1 dozen

<u>**Per Cake:**</u>
Calories: 119
Fat: 1 gram
Carbohydrate: 27 grams
Protein: 2 grams
Cholesterol: 0 milligrams
Sodium: 61 milligrams
Dietary Fiber: 2 grams

Orange Pancakes

1 cup whole wheat flour
1 teaspoon Rumford aluminum-
   free baking powder
1/4 teaspoon cinnamon
1 egg white

1/2 cup fresh orange juice
1/2 cup nonfat plain yogurt
1/2 teaspoon canola oil
Vegetable cooking spray

Combine first 3 ingredients in a medium-sized mixing bowl. Set aside.

Combine next 4 ingredients in a smaller bowl and beat together.

Add liquid to the dry ingredients and stir until flour is moistened.

Spoon batter onto a hot griddle that has been lightly sprayed with cooking spray. Cook until golden brown on both sides.

Serve with orange syrup, (see recipe), pourable fruit, pure maple syrup, or unsweetened applesauce.

Yield: 4 servings

Per Serving:
Calories: 140
Fat: 1 gram
Carbohydrate: 27 grams
Protein: 7 grams
Cholesterol: 0 milligrams
Sodium: 124 milligrams
Dietary Fiber: 4 grams

Outstanding Oats

1/2 cup old-fashioned rolled oats,
    uncooked
1 tablespoon raisins or currants
Boiling distilled water
6 raw almonds, chopped
1 tablespoon plain nonfat yogurt
1 medium apple, grated

Combine oats and raisins and add just enough boiling water to cover. Allow to soak for 4-5 minutes.
Add remaining ingredients and stir.
Yield: 1-2 servings

Per Serving:
Calories: 323
Fat: 6 grams
Carbohydrate: 51 grams
Protein: 10 grams
Cholesterol: 0 milligrams
Sodium: 12 milligrams
Dietary Fiber: 8 grams

Orange Pancake and Waffle Syrup

(Try the variation to make other fresh fruit syrups).

2 cups fresh orange juice
1 tablespoon lemon juice
1/4 cup brown rice syrup or
    raw honey
1 tablespoon cornstarch or
    arrowroot powder
1 tablespoon water

Simmer first 3 ingredients over medium low heat for 5 minutes.
Add cornstarch that has been dissolved in 1 tablespoon water and simmer until thick, stirring constantly, about 3 minutes.
Yield: 2 cups

Variation: Omit the orange juice and substitute 1/2 cup water with honey and lemon juice. Then add 2 cups fresh blueberries or strawberries and simmer 10 minutes before adding cornstarch mixture.

Per Tablespoon:
Calories: 13
Fat: 0 grams
Carbohydrate: 3 grams
Protein: 0 grams
Cholesterol: 0 milligrams
Sodium: 0 milligrams
Dietary Fiber: 0 grams

Mexican Omelet

1/4 cup egg beaters
2-3 tablespoons chopped green pepper
1 tablespoon mild salsa
1/8 cup (1/2 ounce) reduced-fat Cheddar cheese
Vegetable cooking spray

Spray a nonstick skillet with cooking spray. Heat skillet over medium heat until a drop of water sizzles in the pan.

Add 1/4 egg beaters and tilt pan so that egg beaters forms a circle.

Sprinkle green pepper, salsa, and cheese on top of egg. When cheese is melted and omelet is lightly browned on bottom, lift with a spatula half of the circle and fold it over the other half to form omelet.

Remove from pan and serve with more salsa drizzled on top.
Yield: 1 serving

Per Serving:
Calories: 98
Fat: 5 grams
Carbohydrate: 2 grams
Protein: 12 grams
Cholesterol: 11 milligrams
Sodium: 223 milligrams
Dietary Fiber: 0 grams

Pineapple Cooler

1 ripe banana
1 cup pineapple juice
1/2 cup nonfat plain yogurt
1 teaspoon honey
1 teaspoon vanilla extract

Peel and slice ripe banana. Wrap in wax paper and freeze until firm.

Combine banana and remaining ingredients in a blender and blend until smooth.

Yield: 1 serving

Per Serving:
Calories: 321
Fat: 1 gram
Carbohydrate: 74 grams
Protein: 8 grams
Cholesterol: 3 milligrams
Sodium: 74 milligrams
Dietary Fiber: 3 grams

Spiced Breakfast Millet

1/2 cup millet, washed and drained
2 2/3 cup water
1/4 - 1/2 cup raisins
1/4 teaspoon salt
1/4 teaspoon allspice
Pure maple syrup

Combine all ingredients in small saucepan.
Bring to a boil. Cover, reduce heat, and simmer for 30 minutes or until all liquid is absorbed.
Spoon into serving dishes and pour 1 teaspoon maple syrup over the top.
Serve immediately.
Yield: 4 servings
*Also makes a delicious snack or dessert when garnished with fresh fruit or topped with one of the delicious fruit dessert toppings. (See Special Treats Section)

Per Serving:
Calories: 126
Fat: 1 gram
Carbohydrate: 27 grams
Protein: 3 grams
Cholesterol: 0 milligrams
Sodium: 162 milligrams
Dietary Fiber: 3 grams

Strawberry Pancakes

1 cup whole wheat flour
1/2 teaspoon baking soda
1 teaspoon Rumford aluminum-free baking powder
2 egg whites

1 cup nonfat strawberry yogurt
1/3 cup skim milk
Sliced strawberries
Strawberry pourable fruit syrup

Combine first 3 ingredients in medium-sized mixing bowl. Set aside.

Combine next 3 ingredients, mixing well and add to flour mixture.

Pour batter to form pancakes on preheated nonstick griddle and cook until bubbles appear, about 2 to 3 minutes. Turn and cook other side until lightly browned.

Top with sliced strawberries and syrup.

Yield: 12 (3-inch) pancakes

Per 3 pancake Serving
Calories: 201
Fat: 0 grams
Carbohydrate: 39 grams
Protein: 9 grams
Cholesterol: 3 milligrams
Sodium: 255 milligrams
Dietary Fiber: 3 grams

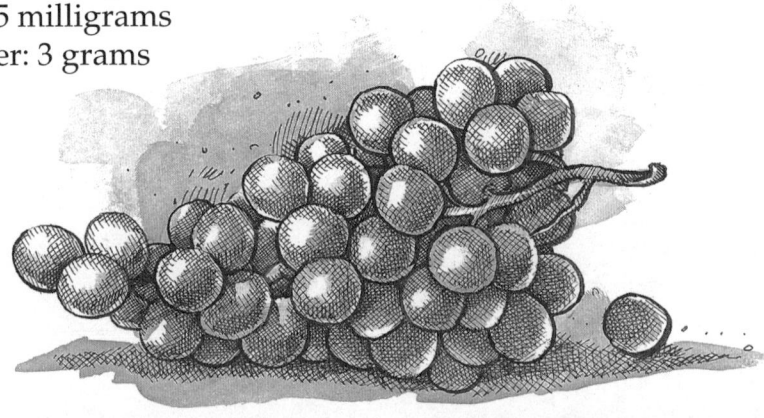

Weekend Breakfast Quiche

3/4 cup whole wheat flour
1/4 cup ground raw almonds
1/2 teaspoon Rumford aluminum-free baking powder
1/4 teaspoon sea salt
1/3 cup skim milk
1 tablespoon canola oil
1 cup egg beaters
1/2 cup chopped onion
1/2 cup chopped tomatoes
1/2 cup finely chopped broccoli florets
1/8 teaspoon pepper
1 tablespoon chopped cilantro or parsley
Vegetable cooking spray

Lightly spray a 9-inch pie pan or quiche dish with cooking spray. Set aside.

Combine first 4 ingredients in a medium-sized bowl. Add milk and oil. Stir until just moistened. Lightly oil your fingers with cooking spray and remove dough from bowl.

Pat out dough evenly onto the bottom and up the sides of the pie pan. Bake at 400 degrees for about 5-6 minutes, or until golden brown. Remove from oven and reduce oven temperature to 375 degrees.

Combine remaining ingredients and pour into baked crust. Bake for 25-30 minutes or until center appears to be set.

Slice and serve with fresh salsa if desired.

Yield: 6 servings

Per Serving:
Calories: 150
Fat: 6 grams
Carbohydrate: 15 grams
Protein: 9 grams
Cholesterol: 0 milligrams
Sodium: 214 milligrams

Dietary Fiber: 3 grams

Whole Wheat Waffles

(Try doubling this recipe. They always go in a hurry at our house! If you have any leftovers, they freeze well for later).

1 1/4 cups whole wheat flour
1 tablespoon baking powder
1/4 teaspoon sea salt
1 1/4 cups nonfat buttermilk

2 tablespoons molasses
1/4 cup egg beaters
2 egg whites
Vegetable cooking spray

Combine first 3 ingredients in large bowl.
Combine next 3 ingredients; stirring well. Add to dry mixture and stir until mixture is smooth.
Beat egg whites until stiff peak forms. Gently fold into batter.
Spray an 8-inch square nonstick waffle iron with cooking spray. Allow to preheat.
Pour about 1 cup batter onto hot waffle iron. Close lid and cook until light goes off. Repeat with remaining batter.
Yield: 4-6 servings

Per Serving:
Calories: 139
Fat: 1 gram
Carbohydrate: 26 grams
Protein: 8 grams
Cholesterol: 2 milligrams
Sodium: 373 milligrams
Dietary Fiber: 3 grams

CHAPTER THREE
Sweet Breads Muffins & Cookies

"For lo, the winter is past, the rain is over and gone. The flowers appear on the earth; The time of singing has come, And the voice of the turtledove is heard in our land. The fig tree puts forth her green figs, and the vines with the tender grapes give a good smell. Rise up, my love my fair one, and come away!"

(Song of Solomon 2:11-13)

Almond Raspberry Tortes

1 cup almonds, ground in blender
1 cup oatmeal, buzzed in blender
1 cup whole wheat flour,
   *(or spelt flour)
1/2 teaspoon cinnamon
Pinch of salt

1/2 cup canola oil
1/2 cup pure maple syrup
(or brown rice syrup)
Raspberry all fruit jam

Combine first 5 ingredients in large mixing bowl, blending well.

Combine oil and syrup, then add to flour mixture; stirring well.

Roll small amounts of dough in the palms of your hands into little balls and place on ungreased cookie sheet. With your fingers make a small indention in the center of each cookie and add about 1/2 teaspoon raspberry jam.

Bake at 350 degrees for 15 minutes until lightly browned.

Yield: 3 dozen

*I like to use spelt flour because it is not as heavy as whole wheat flour.

**Even though these cookies are not low in fat, they contain wholesome, natural ingredients and make an excellent lunchbox treat for children or a great snack for after school. For children we are concerned with providing healthy treats and snacks containing the "good fats" instead of severely limiting their fat intake.

Per Cookie:
Calories: 98
Carbohydrate: 8 grams
Cholesterol: 0 milligrams
Dietary Fiber: 1 grams

Fat: 6 grams
Protein: 2 grams
Sodium: 9 milligrams

Applesauce Muffins

1 cup unsweetened applesauce
1/4 cup egg beaters
1/4 cup honey
1 cup whole wheat flour
1 cup unbleached all-
   purpose flour*

2 teaspoons baking powder
3/4 teaspoon baking soda
1/2 teaspoon cinnamon
1/4 teaspoon nutmeg
1 cup raisins
Vegetable cooking spray

   Beat together first 3 ingredients in a large mixing bowl. Set aside.
   Combine flours and next 4 ingredients. Add to applesauce mixture and stir just to moisten the dry ingredients.
   Stir in the raisins and divide the batter among 12 nonstick or greased muffin cups.
   Bake at 375 degrees for about 20 minutes.
   Yield: 12 muffins

*Note: You may use all whole wheat flour or substitute both flours with spelt flour.

Per Muffin:
Calories: 146
Fat: 0 grams
Carbohydrate: 34 grams
Protein: 4 grams
Cholesterol: 0 milligrams
Sodium: 92 milligrams
Dietary Fiber: 2 grams

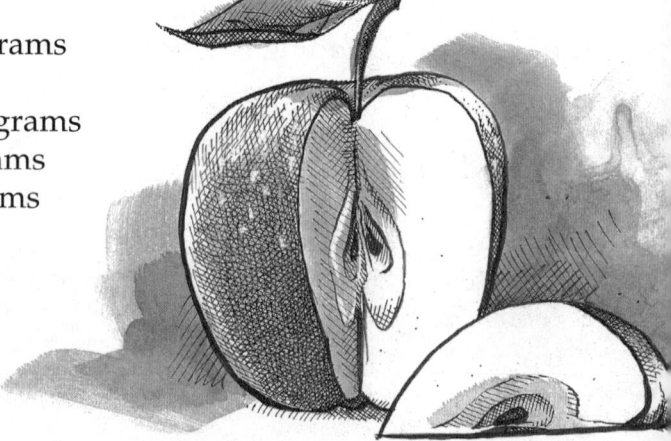

Applesauce-Raisin Bread

1 cup rolled oats,
   (old-fashioned kind)
1 cup whole wheat flour*
1 cup all purpose flour
4 teaspoons baking powder**
1/2 teaspoon cinnamon
1/4 teaspoon ground ginger
1/4 teaspoon ground cloves

1/4 teaspoon sea salt
1/4 cup egg beaters
1/2 cup brown rice syrup (or
   1/3 cup maple syrup)
3/4 cup unsweetened
   applesauce
1/2 cup distilled water
1 cup raisins
Vegetable cooking spray

   Buzz rolled oats in blender 1-2 minutes til they resemble flour. Combine oats and next 7 ingredients in large mixing bowl. Set aside.
   Beat together egg substitute and next 3 ingredients until they are well blended. Stir in raisins.
   Add applesauce mixture to flour, stirring the mixture until the flour is just moistened.
   Pour into a 9 x 5 x 3-inch loaf pan that has been lightly sprayed with cooking spray.
   Bake at 350 degrees for 50-60 minutes or until a toothpick or knife inserted in the center of the loaf comes out clean. Let bread cool 10 minutes in pan and then remove onto a rack to cool completely.
   Yield: 1 loaf (approximately 24 slices)

Note: *Spelt flour may always be used in place of whole wheat and all-purpose flour.
    **Always use an aluminum-free baking powder, ie: Rumford's.

Per Slice:
Calories: 85
Carbohydrate: 19 grams
Cholesterol: 0 milligrams
Dietary Fiber: 1 gram

Fat: 0 grams
Protein: 2 grams
Sodium: 31 milligrams

Best-Ever Bran Muffins

3 cups shredded bran cereal, (i.e., All-Bran, 100% Bran)
1 cup raisins
1 cup boiling water
1/2 cup applesauce, unsweetened
1/2 cup egg beaters
2 cups nonfat buttermilk
1/4 cup molasses
4 teaspoons honey
2 1/4 cups whole wheat flour
2 1/2 teaspoons baking soda
1/2 teaspoon sea salt
Vegetable cooking spray

Combine cereal and raisins. Pour the boiling water over them. Set aside to cool slightly.

Combine next 5 ingredients, mixing well, and add to partly cooled cereal mixture.

Combine flour, baking soda, and salt and add to cereal mixture, stirring just enough to moisten the dry ingredients. Cover with plastic wrap or a damp towel and let batter stand for about 1 hour.

Spray 24 muffin cups with vegetable cooking spray or use nonstick muffin pans. Divide the batter evenly among the muffin cups.

Bake at 400 degrees for 20-25 minutes.

Yield: 24 muffins

Per Muffin:
Calories: 96
Fat: 0 grams
Carbohydrate: 23 grams
Protein: 4 grams
Cholesterol: 0 milligrams
Sodium: 248 miligrams
Dietary Fiber: 2 grams

Chewy Apple-Oat Bars

2 cups rolled oats
   (old-fashioned kind)
1 teaspoon cinnamon
3/4 cup raisins
3 cups peeled and coarsely
   grated apples (about 5)
1/4 cup real maple syrup or
   thawed, frozen apple
   juice concentrate
2 teaspoons vanilla extract
1 1/4 cups whole wheat flour
Vegetable cooking spray

Mix together first 3 ingredients.

Add apples and any juice that collected when grating to the oat mixture.

Add maple syrup, or apple juice concentrate, and vanilla and mix well. Let mixture stand for 10 minutes.

Mix flour into apple-oat mixture. Press out dough evenly onto an 11 x 17-inch nonstick cooking sheet that has been lightly sprayed with cooking spray.

Bake at 350 degrees for 25 minutes. Allow to cool and cut into bars.

Store in plastic bags in the refrigerator. (These bars also freeze nicely)!

Yield: 30 bars

Per Bar:
Calories: 63
Fat: 1 gram
Carbohydrate: 15 grams
Protein: 2 grams
Cholesterol: 0 milligrams
Sodium: 1 milligram
Dietary Fiber: 2 grams

Cranberry Muffins

1 1/2 cups yellow cornmeal, preferably coarse ground
1 1/4 cups whole wheat flour, (or spelt flour)
1 teaspoon cinnamon
1/3 cup orange juice
3/4 cup brown rice syrup, or maple syrup
3 large apples
1 1/2 cups fresh raw cranberries
1 teaspoon baking soda
Vegetable cooking spray

Combine cornmeal, flour, and cinnamon in a large mixing bowl. Set aside.

Combine orange juice and syrup in a small mixing bowl.

Core apples but do not peel. Place them in a food processor and process until the apple is in small bits. (If you do not have a food processor, use a blender or chop into very small pieces.)

Add orange juice mixture and apple bits to the cornmeal mixture and beat until well mixed. (The batter will be very thick.)

Fold in cranberries.

Sprinkle baking soda over the batter and **quickly** mix in.

Drop batter into muffin tins that have been lightly sprayed with vegetable cooking spray.

Bake in a 400 degree oven for 30 minutes.

Yield: 12 muffins

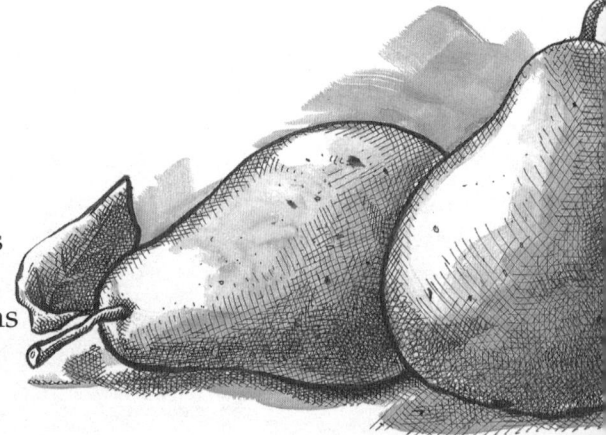

Per Muffin:
Calories: 211
Fat: 1 gram
Carbohydrate: 50 grams
Protein: 3 grams
Cholesterol: 0 milligrams
Sodium: 108 milligrams
Dietary Fiber: 5 grams

SWEET BREADS, MUFFINS & COOKIES

Julie's Gingerbread

2 1/2 cups whole wheat flour*
1 cup molasses, mild flavor
3/4 cup hot water
1/2 cup applesauce
1/4 egg beaters

1 teaspoon baking soda
1 teaspoon ground ginger
1 teaspoon ground cinnamon
3/4 teaspoon sea salt
Vegetable cooking spray

Combine all ingredients, except cooking spray, in a large mixing bowl. Beat 30 seconds at low speed then 3 minutes at medium speed.

Spray an 8x8 glass baking dish with cooking spray. Pour batter into dish and bake at 325 degrees for 50 minutes.

Cool, cut into squares, and serve.

Yield: 16 servings

*__Option:__ For lighter gingerbread you may use 1 1/2 cups whole wheat flour and 1 cup unbleached all-purpose flour

Per Serving:
Calories: 121
Fat: 0 grams
Carbohydrate: 28 grams
Protein: 3 grams
Cholesterol: 0 milligrams
Sodium: 87 milligrams
Dietary Fiber: 2 grams

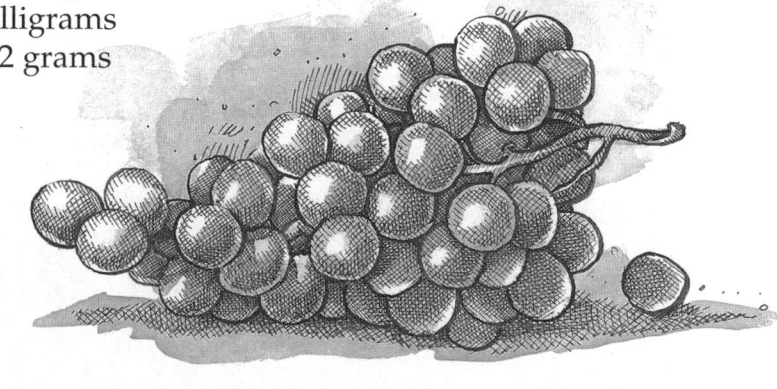

Lemon Biscuits

2 cups whole wheat flour
1 1/2 teaspoons grated lemon peel
1 tablespoon Rumford aluminum-free baking powder
1 1/2 teaspoons baking soda
1 tablespoon poppy seeds
1 tablespoon honey
1 cup nonfat lemon-flavored yogurt
1/4 cup nonfat buttermilk
2 tablespoons applesauce

Combine first 5 ingredients; mix well. Set aside.
Combine remaining ingredients. Make a well in center of flour mixture and add yogurt mixture. Stir to blend. (Dough will be very moist.)
Turn dough onto a lightly floured surface and gently knead 8-10 minutes, adding flour as needed.
Pat dough to 1/2-inch thickness. Cut dough with a 2-inch biscuit cutter and place on a nonstick baking sheet.
Bake at 450 degrees for 10-12 minutes or until lightly browned.
Yield: 12-14 biscuits

Per Biscuit:
Calories: 81
Fat: 0 grams
Carbohydrate: 17 grams
Protein: 3 grams
Cholesterol: 0 milligrams
Sodium: 61 milligrams
Dietary Fiber: 2 grams

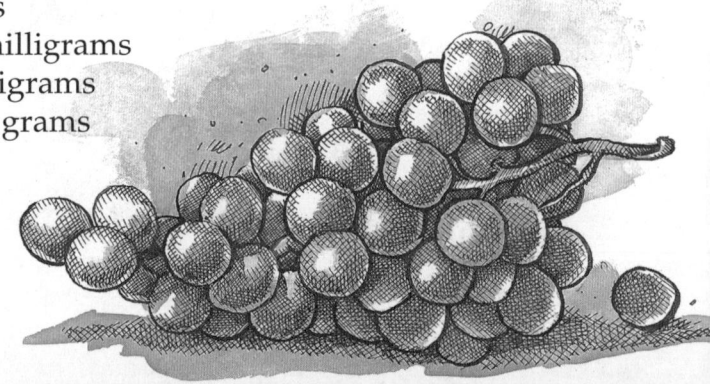

Oatmeal Banana Cookies

1 cup mashed ripe banana
2 egg whites
1 cup chopped dates
1 1/2 cups old-fashioned rolled oats
1/2 cup raisins
Dash of salt
1 teaspoon vanilla

Combine banana and egg whites in large mixing bowl.
Stir in dates and mix until the dates are separating from each other.
Stir in oats and let mixture stand for 15 minutes to allow flavors to mingle.
Drop by teaspoonfuls onto a nonstick baking sheet.
Bake at 350 degrees for 20 minutes or until golden.
Yield: 2 dozen

Per Cookie:
Calories: 59
Fat: 0 grams
Carbohydrate: 13 grams
Protein: 1 gram
Cholesterol: 0 milligrams
Sodium: 17 milligrams
Dietary Fiber: 1 gram

Oatmeal Raisin Cookies

2 cups whole wheat or spelt flour
2 cups old-fashioned rolled oats
1 teaspoon baking soda
1 teaspoon baking powder
1 teaspoon cinnamon
Dash of Salt

1 cup brown rice syrup
1 teaspoon vanilla
1 cup raisins
1/2 cup egg beaters
1/4 cup applesauce

Combine first 6 ingredients in large mixing bowl and mix well. Set aside.

Combine remaining ingredients in medium mixing bowl and stir well.

Gently stir liquid ingredients into flour mixture just until flour is moistened.

Drop heaping teaspoonfuls of dough onto nonstick cookie sheet. Using the back of spoon, slightly press down each cookie.

Bake at 350 degrees for 10-12 minutes.

Yield: 3 1/2 dozen

Per Cookie:
Calories: 95
Fat: 0 grams
Carbohydrate: 22 grams
Protein: 2 grams
Cholesterol: 0 milligrams
Sodium: 92 milligrams
Dietary Fiber: 2 grams

Orange Muffins
(These are great breakfast muffins!
Serve with apple butter and fresh fruit.)

2 cups whole wheat flour
2 teaspoons baking powder
1/2 teaspoon baking soda
1/8 teaspoon sea salt
1/4 cup egg beaters

1/4 cup unsweetened applesauce
1 1/2 cups orange juice, preferably fresh
1 teaspoon grated orange zest
1 cup raisins

Combine first 4 ingredients in large bowl. Set aside.
Combine next 4 ingredients; stirring well.
Add liquid to flour mixture and stir just until flour is moistened.
Fold in raisins and divide batter among 12 muffin cups. (Use a nonstick muffin pan.)
Bake at 375 degrees for about 20 minutes, testing with a toothpick to see when they are fully baked. (Do not overbake.)
Yield: 12 muffins

Per Muffin:
Calories: 125
Fat: 0 grams
Carbohydrate: 28 grams
Protein: 4 grams
Cholesterol: 0 milligrams
Sodium: 89 milligrams
Dietary Fiber: 3 grams

Sweet Corn Muffins

1 cup whole wheat flour
1 cup yellow corn meal
4 teaspoons baking powder
1/2 teaspoon sea salt
1/4 cup honey (or brown
   rice syrup)
1/4 cup egg beaters

Pinch of baking soda
1 cup buttermilk
3 tablespoons unsweetened
   applesauce
1/4 cup nonfat yogurt
1/2 cup corn kernels*

Combine first 4 ingredients in large mixing bowl. Set aside.

Combine remaining ingredients in separate bowl; mixing well. Add to the flour mixture, stirring just until dry ingredients are moistened.

Spoon batter into 12 muffin cups that have been lightly sprayed with cooking spray.

Bake at 425 degrees for 20 to 25 minutes or until the tops are golden and the muffins test done with a toothpick.

Yield: 12 muffins

*****Note:** I used frozen corn that had thawed a little and then I drained any excess water. You could also use canned corn kernels that have been drained.

Per Muffin:
Calories: 130
Fat: 1 gram
Carbohydrate: 27 grams
Protein: 5 grams
Cholesterol: 1 milligram
Sodium: 192 milligrams
Dietary Fiber: 2 grams

CHAPTER FOUR

Soups

"And Jacob gave Esau bread and stew of lentils; then he ate and drank, arose, and went his way."

(Genesis 25:34)

Best-Ever Chicken and Rice Soup

12 cups water
2-3 large boneless, skinless
   chicken breast halves
2 stalks celery
1 small onion, cut into chunks
1 cup chopped onion
1 cup sliced celery
1 cup sliced carrots
1/4 cup fresh parsley, chopped and pressed down
1/2 teaspoon ground pepper
1/2-3/4 teaspoon dried
   thyme leaves
3/4 cup uncooked brown rice
1 bay leaf
2 tablespoons fresh lime
   juice

Combine first 4 ingredients in large Dutch oven and bring to a boil.

Cover, reduce heat, and simmer over medium-low heat until chicken is done, about 20-30 minutes. Remove chicken, cool, and chop to equal 2 cups. Set aside.

Strain broth; discarding onion and celery. Return broth to Dutch oven.

Add remaining ingredients to chicken broth, except for lime juice, and bring to a boil. Cover, reduce heat, and simmer for 20 minutes.

Add chopped chicken and continue to cook until rice is tender, about 20 more minutes.

After soup has cooked, stir in lime juice and serve.

Yield: 8 servings

Per Serving:
Calories: 139
Carbohydrate: 19 grams
Sodium: 87 milligrams
Dietary Fiber: 2 grams
Fat: 3 grams
Protein: 8 grams
Cholesterol: 26 milligrams

Broccoli Bisque

1 cup diced onion
1 large garlic clove, chopped
2 tablespoons plus 4 cups
　　fat-free chicken broth
1 package (16-ounce) frozen
　　broccoli florets, thawed
1/2 cup plain nonfat yogurt
Sea salt and pepper to taste

Saute onion and garlic in 2 tablespoons chicken broth for 5 minutes or until lightly browned, stirring often.

Add 4 cups chicken broth and bring to a boil. Add broccoli; reduce heat to low and simmer 7 minutes or until tender.

Cool slightly and pour mixture into large blender or food processor. Puree until smooth.

Reserve 2 tablespoons yogurt; blend in remaining yogurt until smooth.

Serve in bowls; swirl in reserved yogurt.

Yield: 6 servings

Per Serving:
Calories: 37
Fat: 0 grams
Carbohydrate: 6 grams
Protein: 3 grams
Cholesterol: 0 milligrams
Sodium: 614 milligrams
Dietary Fiber: 0 grams

Cabbage Soup

2 tablespoons fat-free, low sodium chicken broth
2 cloves garlic, minced
1 large onion, chopped
3 carrots, diced
1 stalk chopped celery, including leaves
1 head cabbage, chopped
5 red potatoes, cubed
2 quarts vegetable or fat-free, low sodium chicken broth
1/2 teaspoon parsley
Salt and pepper to taste

Saute garlic, onion, carrots, celery, and cabbage in 2 tablespoons chicken broth in Dutch oven.

Add potatoes, 2 quarts chicken broth, and parsley. Cook for 1 hour.

Yield: 6 servings

Per Serving:
Calories: 317
Fat: 2 grams
Carbohydrate: 69 grams
Protein: 12 grams
Cholesterol: 0 milligrams
Sodium: 920 milligrams
Dietary Fiber: 14 grams

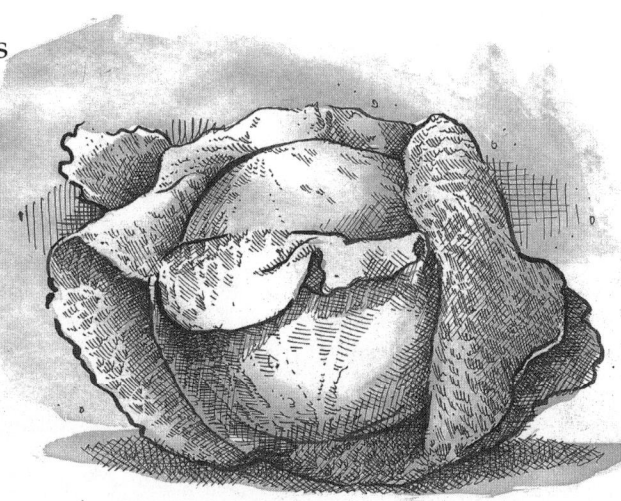

Easy Black Bean Soup

(This same delicious recipe may be used with split peas, garbanzo beans or any other bean of your choice.)

2 1/2 cups dried black beans
2 (16 ounce) cans fat-free chicken broth
1 bay leaf
6 cloves garlic
1 large green pepper, chopped
1 large tomato, chopped
1 medium onion, chopped
2 teaspoons olive oil

Place dried black beans in large Dutch oven. Cover with water 1-2 inches above beans. Soak 24-48 hours. Rinse and drain beans.

Combine soaked beans, chicken broth, and bay leaf in Dutch oven.

Place tomato, green pepper, garlic, and onion in a blender and blend until smooth.

Heat olive oil in large saucepan and add vegetable mixture.

Saute for 5-7 minutes over medium heat; then add to black beans.

Bring beans to a boil, cover, reduce heat, and simmer for 3 hours or until beans are tender. (You could prepare ingredients and cook in a crock pot on low all day.)

Serve over rice with any or all of the following: fresh chives, salsa, nonfat sour cream.

Yield: 8 servings

Per Serving:
Calories: 246
Fat: 2 grams
Carbohydrate: 44 grams
Protein: 14 grams
Cholesterol: 0 milligrams
Sodium: 403 milligrams
Dietary Fiber: 10 grams

Great 9 Bean Soup

2 cups 9 Bean Soup Mix (see below)
2 quarts nonfat chicken broth
1 large onion, chopped
2 cloves garlic, minced
1 teaspoon sea salt
2 cans stewed tomatoes,
    Del Monte Original Recipe (no salt)

Place 2 cups 9 Bean Soup Mix in a Dutch oven or large pot and cover with water 2 inches above beans. Soak 24-48 hours for best results. Drain beans and return to Dutch oven.

Add nonfat chicken broth and remaining ingredients; stir.

Bring to a boil, cover, reduce heat, and simmer for 2-3 hours. Stir occasionally. (For a thicker soup, remove 1/4 of the soup and blend in a blender. Return to pot and mix.)

Yield: 8 servings

Per Serving:
Calories: 104
Carbohydrate: 21 grams
Cholesterol: 0 milligrams
Dietary Fiber: 3 grams
Fat: 1 gram
Protein: 6 grams
Sodium: 400 milligrams

9 Bean Soup Mix
(Mix 1 dry cup of each of the following:)

Black-Eyed Peas
Black Beans
Red Kidney Beans
Pinto Beans
Great Northern Beans
Split Peas
Lentils
Navy Beans
Barley Pearls

Lentil-Barley Soup

1 tablespoon olive oil
3/4 cup chopped celery
3/4 cup chopped onion
2 cloves garlic, minced
6 cups water or fat-free
    chicken broth
3/4 cup lentils, soaked and rinsed

4 cups canned tomatoes
3/4 cup barley
1 teaspoon sea salt
1/4 teaspoon pepper
1/8-1/4 teaspoon rosemary
1/2 cup shredded carrots

Saute celery, onion, and garlic in olive oil.
Add water and lentils and cook 20 minutes.
Add next 5 ingredients and cook 50-60 minutes.
Add shredded carrots. Cook 5 more minutes and serve.
Yield: 6 servings

Per Serving:
Calories: 260
Fat: 3 grams
Carbohydrate: 41 grams
Protein: 12 grams
Cholesterol: 0 milligrams
Sodium: 671 milligrams
Dietary Fiber: 14 grams

Lentil-Rice Soup

(With the rice and lentils in this recipe you have the protein quality of beef without the cost or the fat. It also freezes well!*)

5 cups fat-free chicken broth
3 cups water
1 1/2 cups lentils, **soaked and rinsed
1 cup uncooked brown rice
1 large can diced tomatoes, (35-ounce)
3 carrots; halved lengthwise, then sliced
1 cup onion, chopped
2 tablespoons apple cider vinegar
1 large celery stalk, chopped
3 large cloves garlic, minced
1/2 teaspoon dried basil
1/2 teaspoon dried oregano
1/2 teaspoon dried thyme
1 bay leaf
1/2 cup fresh parsley, chopped
Sea salt and pepper to taste

Combine all ingredients except parsley, vinegar, salt, and pepper in large Dutch oven.
Bring soup to a boil. Cover, reduce heat, and simmer soup for 45-55 minutes until the lentils and rice are both tender.
Remove bay leaf and stir in parsley, vinegar, salt and pepper. (If necessary, thin soup to desired consistency with additional broth.)
Yield: 8 servings

Note: *When making soup to freeze, do not add parsley and vinegar. It should be added after the soup has been thawed and reheated.)
**I like to soak my lentils 24 hours before cooking to eliminate some of the gas.

Per Serving:
Calories: 260
Carbohydrate: 49 grams
Cholesterol: 0 milligrams
Dietary Fiber: 14 grams
Fat: 2 grams
Protein: 14 grams
Sodium: 400 milligrams

Luscious Lentil Soup

1 tablespoon olive oil
2 cups chopped onion
3 medium carrots, coarsely grated
3/4 teaspoon marjoram
3/4 teaspoon thyme
1 (28-ounce) can dice tomatoes
7 cups nonfat chicken or vegetable broth
1 1/2 cups lentils, soaked and rinsed
1/2 teaspoon sea salt
1/4 teaspoon pepper
6 ounces dry white wine
1/3 cup fresh parsley, chopped
4 ounces reduced-fat Cheddar cheese (optional)

Saute onions, carrots, marjoram, and thyme in olive oil for about 5 minutes.

Add next 3 ingredients and bring to a boil. Cover, reduce heat, and simmer the soup for about 1 hour until the lentils are tender.

Add salt, pepper, wine, and parsley and simmer about 5-7 minutes.

Serve soup with cheese sprinkled on top.

Yield: 8 servings

Per Serving:
Calories: 248
Fat: 5 grams
Carbohydrate: 33 grams
Protein: 17 grams
Cholesterol: 10 milligrams
Sodium: 700 milligrams
Dietary Fiber: 13 grams

Minestrone Soup

1 cup finely chopped onion
1/2 cup chopped celery
6 cups vegetable broth or fat-free chicken broth
2 medium zucchini, cubed
1/2 cup chopped fresh parsley
1 cup finely shredded cabbage
1 (20-ounce) can cannelloni beans, rinsed and drained
1 cup uncooked elbow macaroni
1 clove garlic, minced
1/2 teaspoon pepper
1 (16-ounce) can tomatoes, undrained

Saute onion and celery in large Dutch oven in 2 tablespoons chicken broth until tender.

Add remaining ingredients and bring to a boil. Reduce heat and simmer, uncovered, about 30 minutes.

Yield: 8 servings

Per Serving:
Calories: 186
Fat: 1 gram
Carbohydrate: 36 grams
Protein: 10 grams
Cholesterol: 0 milligrams
Sodium: 734 milligrams
Dietary Fiber: 6 grams

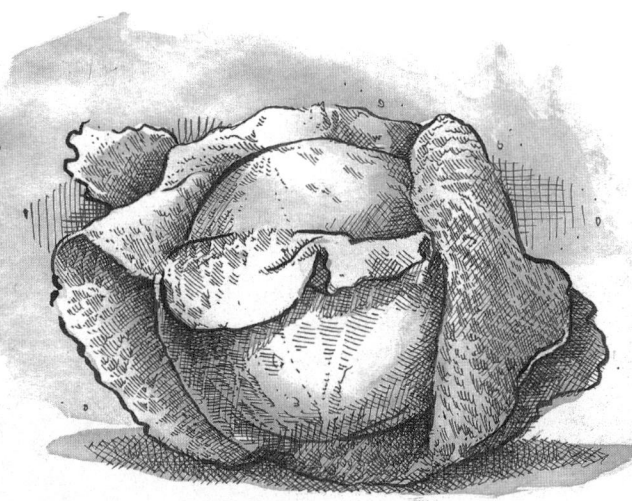

Fat-Free Chicken Broth

8 cups distilled water
3 pounds chicken parts,
   wings, ribs, etc.
1 large onion, quartered
2 stalks celery, cut in chunks

Combine all ingredients in large pot. Bring to a boil, reduce heat, cover, and simmer for 1-2 hours.

Remove chicken and strain broth through a mesh strainer into a large bowl or pot.

Cover broth and refrigerate; allowing fat to rise to the top of the broth and congeal. Skim off fat layer and discard.

Refrigerate broth or freeze for later use. Try freezing broth in ice cube trays and store cubes in a freezer bag. This way you have access to small amounts of broth. Most ice cube trays hold approximately 2 tablespoons per section.

Yield: 2 quarts

Per 1 Cup Serving:
Calories: 185
Fat: 0 grams
Carbohydrate: 2 grams
Protein: 41 grams
Cholesterol: 0 milligrams
Sodium: 123 milligrams
Dietary Fiber: 0 grams

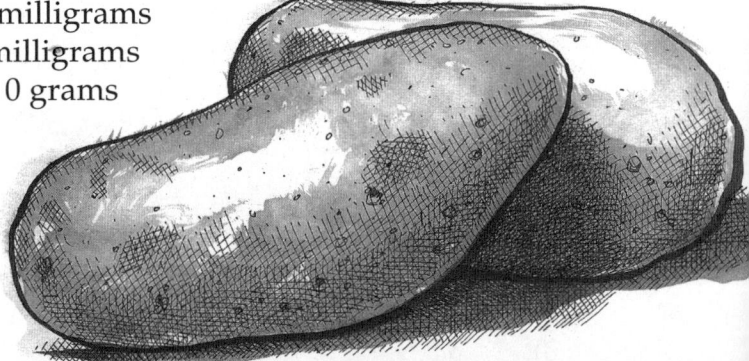

Potato-Bean Soup

1/2 cup sliced celery
2 medium carrots, shredded
1 clove garlic, minced
2 teaspoons olive oil
4 cups fat-free chicken broth
3 medium potatoes, peeled
    and cut up

2 tablespoons fresh dill
1 (15 ounce) can great
    northern beans, drained
1/2 cup plain nonfat yogurt
    or nonfat sour cream
1 tablespoon flour
1/8 teaspoon pepper

Saute first 3 ingredients in large saucepan in olive oil over medium heat until tender, about 4 minutes.

Stir in chicken broth, potatoes, and dill. Bring to a boil; reduce heat.

Simmer, covered, for 20-25 minutes until potatoes are tender. With back of spoon, mash about half of the potatoes in the broth.

Add drained beans to the broth.

Stir together yogurt, flour, and pepper in small bowl.

Add to potato mixture and cook and stir until thickened.

Yield: 4 servings

Per Serving:
Calories: 325
Fat: 3 grams
Carbohydrate: 60 grams
Protein: 17 grams
Cholesterol: 1 milligram
Sodium: 860 milligrams
Dietary Fiber: 6 grams

Potato Leek Soup

3 large leeks, white and
   light green parts only
1 tablespoon olive oil
4-6 medium potatoes,
   peeled and cubed
2 cans fat-free chicken broth*
2 cups water*
3 tablespoons chopped fresh
   chives
Sea salt and pepper to taste

Saute leeks in large saucepan in olive oil until tender.

Add next two ingredients; bring to a boil. Cover, reduce heat and simmer until potatoes are tender, about 30 minutes.

Puree 1/3 mixture in blender or food processor. (Repeat with remaining potato mixture, if desired. It depends on the texture you want.)

Return to saucepan and add 3 tablespoons chives and salt and pepper to taste. Reheat, stirring constantly until mixture just comes to a boil. Serve immediately.

Yield: 6 servings

*Option: Use 6 cups of water instead of chicken broth.

Per Serving:
Calories: 174
Fat: 3 grams
Carbohydrate: 33 grams
Protein: 7 grams
Cholesterol: 0 milligrams
Sodium: 414 milligrams
Dietary Fiber: 1 gram

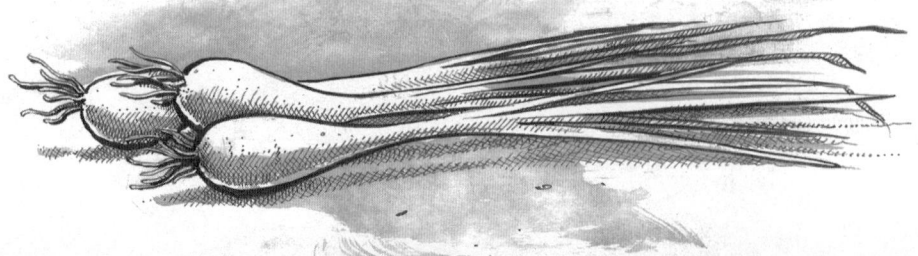

SOUPS

Potato-Yogurt Soup

1 small onion, sliced
3 green onions, sliced
1 clove garlic, crushed
1 teaspoon olive oil
2 tablespoons fat-free chicken broth

2 medium potatoes, sliced
2 cups fat-free chicken broth
1/4 to 1/2 teaspoon dried rosemary
1 (8-ounce) carton plain nonfat yogurt

Saute onions and garlic in olive oil and 3 tablespoons chicken broth in a Dutch oven over medium-high heat until tender.

Add potatoes and 2 cups chicken broth. Bring to a boil over medium heat.

Cover, reduce heat, and simmer about 15 minutes or until potatoes are tender.

Spoon potato mixture and rosemary into a blender. Process until smooth.

Return to Dutch oven and cook over low heat until thoroughly heated.

Stir in yogurt with a wire whisk. Serve immediately.

Yield: 3 servings

Per Servings:
Calories: 196
Fat: 3 grams
Carbohydrate: 32 grams
Protein: 10 grams
Cholesterol: 2 milligrams
Sodium: 614 milligrams
Dietary Fiber: 1 gram

Spinach-Lentil Soup

1 cup dry lentils*
1 medium onion, chopped
1 cup celery, chopped
1 cup sliced carrot
5 cups water
2 cups chopped fresh spinach

2 cloves garlic, minced
1/2 teaspoon grated lemon peel
1/8 teaspoon red pepper (optional)

Combine all ingredients except spinach and bring to a boil. Reduce heat, cover, and simmer for 45 minutes to 1 hour or until lentils are tender.
Stir in spinach and serve.
Yield: 6 servings

*Note: I soak my lentils at least 24 hours, then rinse and drain before using in this recipe.

Per Serving:
Calories: 133
Fat: 0 grams
Carbohydrate: 24 grams
Protein: 10 grams
Cholesterol: 0 milligrams
Sodium: 60 milligrams
Dietary Fiber: 12 grams

Tomato-Rice Soup

2 lbs fresh, ripe tomatoes cored and chopped
1/2 cup uncooked brown rice
1 cup chopped celery
1/2 cup chopped onion
1/4 cup fresh basil, chopped
Salt and pepper to taste
3 tablespoons tomato paste
2 cloves garlic, chopped
1 tablespoon brown rice syrup
1 bay leaf
1 quart water or fat-free chicken broth

Combine all ingredients in large Dutch oven.
Bring to a boil over medium heat, cover, reduce heat and simmer for 30-45 minutes, stirring occasionally.
Remove from heat and allow to cool, about 30 minutes.
Transfer soup to a food processor or blender, in 2 batches if necessary, and process until pureed.
Return to Dutch oven and reheat, if necessary, and serve.
Yield: 4 servings

Per Serving:
Calories: 166
Fat: 2 grams
Carbohydrate: 36 grams
Protein: 5 grams
Cholesterol: 0 milligrams
Sodium: 151 milligrams
Dietary Fiber: 5 grams

Vegetable Barley Soup

2 cans fat-free chicken broth
1 can water
1 (16-ounce) can diced tomatoes
2 large carrots, sliced
1 medium onion, chopped
2 stalks chopped celery, including leaves
1 bay leaf
1/2 cup barley

Combine all ingredients in a large Dutch oven. Bring to a boil; cover, reduce heat, and simmer 1 hour.
Remove bay leaf and serve.
Yield: 6 servings

Per Serving:
Calories: 94
Fat: 0 grams
Carbohydrate: 20 grams
Protein: 3 grams
Cholesterol: 0 milligrams
Sodium: 543 milligrams
Dietary Fiber: 3 grams

Vegetable Stock

5 large onions, halved
10 carrots, halved
8 tomatoes, quartered
2 cloves garlic, whole

5 stalks celery, cubed
1 cup fresh parsley, chopped
2 bay leaves
16 cup water

Combine all ingredients in a large pot. Bring to a boil, cover, reduce heat, and simmer about an hour.

Let stand 30 minutes and then strain. Skim any film off the top of stock.

Chill or freeze for later use.

Yield: 16 cups

Per 1 cup serving:
Calories: 73
Fat: 0 grams
Carbohydrate: 17 grams
Protein: 2 grams
Cholesterol: 0 milligrams
Sodium: 39 milligrams
Dietary Fiber: 4 grams

CHAPTER FIVE

Salads

" For the earth which drinks in the rain that often comes upon it, and bears herbs useful for those by whom it is cultivated, receives blessing from God; "

(Hebrews 6:7)

SALADS

Black Bean and Barley Salad

3/4 cup barley, uncooked
1/4 cup lime juice
2 tablespoons water
1 tablespoon olive oil
1 teaspoon honey
1/2 teaspoon garlic powder
1/4 teaspoon sea salt
1/4 teaspoon pepper
1/4 teaspoon ground cumin
1/4 teaspoon ground red pepper
1 (15-ounce) can black beans, rinsed and drained
Leaf lettuce
1 cup chopped tomato
1/4 cup sliced green onions

Cook barley according to package directions; drain and set aside.

Combine lime juice and the next 8 ingredients in a jar. Cover tightly and shake well.

Pour half of dressing over cooked barley; cover and refrigerate 8 hours, stirring occasionally.

Combine black beans and remaining dressing; cover and refrigerate 8 hours, stirring occasionally.

Spoon barley mixture evenly onto lettuce-lined plates. Top with black beans, tomato, and onions.

Yield: 4 servings

Per Serving:
Calories: 237
Fat: 5 grams
Carbohydrate: 43 grams
Protein: 8 grams
Cholesterol: 0 millligrams
Sodium: 156 milligrams
Dietary Fiber: 10 grams

Carrot-Raisin Salad

1/4 cup raisins
2 tablespoons apple cider vinegar
1 (8-ounce) can unsweetened pineapple tidbits, undrained
Dash of cinnamon
Dash of nutmeg
3/4 pound carrots, scraped and coarsely shredded

Combine raisins and vinegar in a small bowl and let stand 30 minutes. Drain and reserve the vinegar. Set raisins aside.

Drain pineapple, reserving 1/4 cup juice.

Combine reserved pineapple juice and vinegar, cinnamon, and nutmeg.

Pour over raisins, carrots, and pineapple tidbits. Toss well and chill.

Yield: 4 servings

Per Serving:
Calories: 265
Fat: 0 grams
Carbohydrate: 65 grams
Protein: 1 gram
Cholesterol: 0 milligrams
Sodium: 86 milligrams
Dietary Fiber: 3 grams

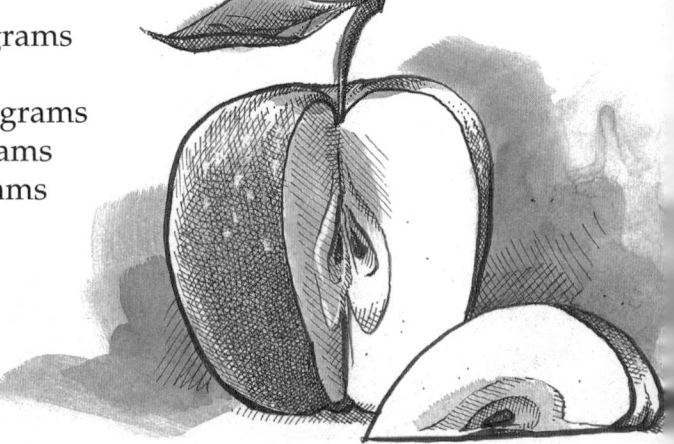

Citrus Marinated Fruit

Fruit:
- 1 cup cantaloupe balls
- 1 cup blueberries
- 1 cup seedless green grapes, halved
- 1 cup strawberries, halved or whole

Orange Marinade:
- 1 tablespoon brown rice syrup
- 3/4 cup orange juice
- 1/4 cup white grape juice
- 2 tablespoons lemon juice

Combine fruit in large bowl.
Combine marinade ingredients; mix well.
Pour marinade over fruit. Cover and refrigerate 2-3 hours to blend flavors. Stir occasionally.
Serve in sherbet glasses as an elegant dessert. Garnish with fresh mint leaves if desired.
Yield: 8 servings

Per 1/2 cup Serving:
Calories: 35
Fat: 0 grams
Carbohydrate: 8 grams
Protein: 1 gram
Cholesterol: 0 milligrams
Sodium: 3 milligrams
Dietary Fiber: 1 gram

Colorful Brown Rice Salad

2 1/4 cups water
1 cup brown rice
1/2 teaspoon sea salt
1 cup thin yellow squash strips
1 cup small broccoli florets
1 cup sliced radishes
1/2 cup sliced green onions
1/4 cup chopped fresh dill
3 tablespoons chopped
    fresh parsley
1 teaspoon grated lemon rind
1/3 cup fresh lemon juice
2 tablespoons olive oil
2 teaspoons Dijon mustard

Combine first 3 ingredients in a saucepan and cook according to package directions. Remove from heat and cool.
   Combine rice, squash strips and the next 6 ingredients. Set aside.
   Combine lemon juice and next 3 ingredients in a jar; cover and shake vigorously. Pour over rice mixture and toss gently.
   Cover and chill for 1 to 2 hours. Garnish with dill sprigs and serve on a bed of steamed yellow squash.
   Yield: 6 servings

Per Serving:
Calories: 174
Fat: 6 grams
Carbohydrate: 28 grams
Protein: 4 grams
Cholesterol: 0 milligrams
Sodium: 259 milligrams
Dietary Fiber: 2 grams

Crunchy Barley Salad

1 2/3 cups fat-free chicken broth
1 1/3 cups water
1 cup barley, rinsed
1 tablespoon olive oil
1 large clove garlic, flattened
1/2 teaspoon salt
1/4 teaspoon pepper
3 tablespoons red wine vinegar
1 cup finely chopped green pepper
1 cup carrot, cut in half length-wise and thinly sliced
1/2 cup chopped red onion
1/2 cup chopped celery
1/4 cup chopped fresh dill
1/4 cup chopped fresh parsley

Bring broth and water to a boil and add barley. Return to a boil, cover, reduce heat to low, and simmer for 40-45 minutes or until the barley is tender. (Add more water as the barley cooks if it absorbs all the liquid before it is done.)

Combine the next 5 ingredients and allow to set while the barley is cooking.

Remove garlic from dressing mixture after the barley has finished cooking and pour the dressing mixture over the barley while it is still hot. Toss to mix well.

Refrigerate the barley for 1 hour or longer, then add the vegetables and herbs before serving, or you can add the vegetables and herbs while the barley is still warm and serve.)

Yield: 8 servings

Per Serving:
Calories: 115
Fat: 2 grams
Carbohydrate: 21 grams
Protein: 4 grams
Cholesterol: 0 milligrams
Sodium: 326 milligrams
Dietary Fiber: 5 grams

Marinated Fresh Fruit Bowl

Fruit:
   1 cup honeydew melon balls
   1 cup watermelon balls
   1 cup cantaloupe melon balls
   2 large peaches, peeled and sliced
   1/2 cup strawberries, halved

Marinade:
   1/2 cup brown rice syrup
   1/4 cup water
   1/4 cup lime juice
   1/4 cup orange juice

Combine rice syrup and water; bring to a boil. Reduce heat; simmer 5 minutes.
Stir in lime juice and orange juice. Cool completely.
Combine fruits in medium serving bowl. Pour marinade over fruit; mix gently.
Cover and refrigerate 1-2 hours to blend flavors.
Yield: 8 servings

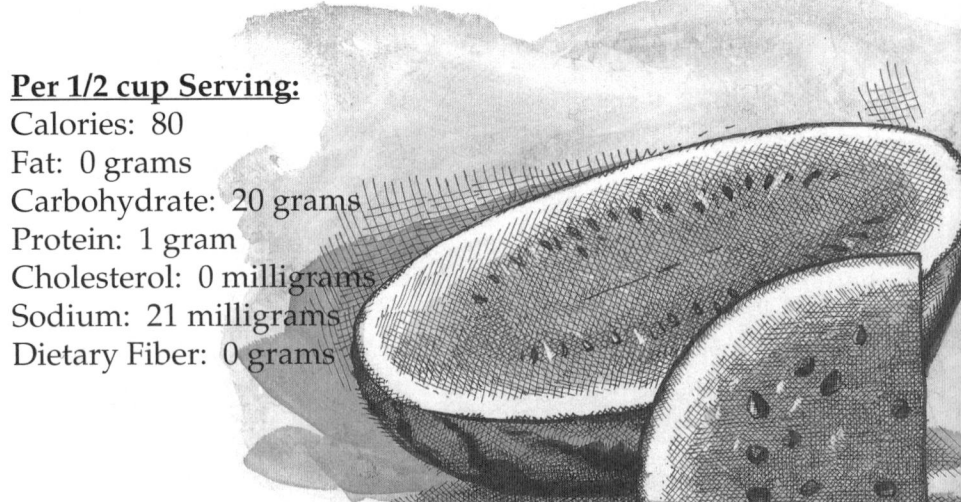

Per 1/2 cup Serving:
Calories: 80
Fat: 0 grams
Carbohydrate: 20 grams
Protein: 1 gram
Cholesterol: 0 milligrams
Sodium: 21 milligrams
Dietary Fiber: 0 grams

Orange Cabbage-Carrot Salad

2 cups finely shredded cabbage
1 1/2 cups shredded carrots
1 1/2 cups coarsely chopped orange sections
1/2 cup raisins
1/4-1/2 cup nonfat vanilla yogurt

Combine all ingredients in a large mixing bowl. Toss gently to coat.
Chill several hours and serve.
Yield: 6 servings

Per Serving:
Calories: 89
Fat: 0 grams
Carbohydrate: 22 grams
Protein: 2 grams
Cholesterol: 0 milligrams
Sodium: 26 milligrams
Dietary Fiber: 3 grams

Rio Grande Quinoa and Corn Salad

(This is a family favorite! Try serving it individually in Crisy Tortilla Bowls.)

3 tablespoons lemon juice
1 tablespoon olive oil
1 tablespoon fresh cilantro, minced
1 1/2 cups water
1 cup fresh or frozen corn
1/2 cup quinoa, uncooked
1/8 teaspoon cumin seeds, toasted (optional)
1 cup black beans, cooked
1 medium tomato, diced
3 tablespoons red onion, finely chopped
Sea salt and pepper to taste

Combine first 3 ingredients in small bowl and set aside.

Bring to a boil in a small saucepan 1 1/2 cups water. Add corn; reduce heat and simmer until corn is tender, about 5-7 minutes. Drain corn and reserve 1 cup cooking liquid. Set aside.

Return 1 cup cooking liquid to saucepan and bring to a boil. Add quinoa and toasted cumin seeds. Cover and simmer about 10 minutes or until liquid is absorbed. Remove quinoa from heat and set aside for 5 minutes.

Fluff quinoa with a fork and transfer to serving bowl. Cool slightly.

Add corn, black beans, tomato and onion to quinoa.

Add olive oil dressing and toss. Chill and serve. (Also, may be served warm.)

Yield: 4 servings

Per Serving:
Calories: 215
Fat: 5 grams
Carbohydrate: 36 grams
Protein: 8 grams
Cholesterol: 0 milligrams
Sodium: 9 milligrams
Dietary Fiber: 7 grams

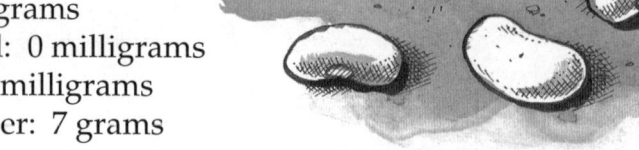

Salmon Pasta Salad

1 cup firmly packed fresh basil leaves
1/4 cup fat-free Italian dressing
2 tablespoons water
3 cloves garlic, crushed
1 pound salmon fillet
1/4 teaspoon pepper
Vegetable cooking spray
4 cups cooked vermicelli
Lemon wedges

Combine first 4 ingredients in food processor. Process for about 2 minutes. Set aside.

Place fillet, skin side down, on a broiler pan coated with cooking spray. Broil 6 inches from heat (with oven door partially open) for 5 minutes. Carefully turn over and broil 4 minutes or until fish flakes. Remove from broiler pan and cool. Break fish into bite-sized pieces.

Combine salmon, basil mixture, and vermicelli in a large bowl. Toss gently and serve with lemon wedges.

Yield: 6 servings

Per Serving:
Calories: 254
Fat: 7 grams
Carbohydrate: 27 grams
Protein: 20 grams
Cholesterol: 49 milligrams
Sodium: 146 milligrams
Dietary Fiber: 1 gram

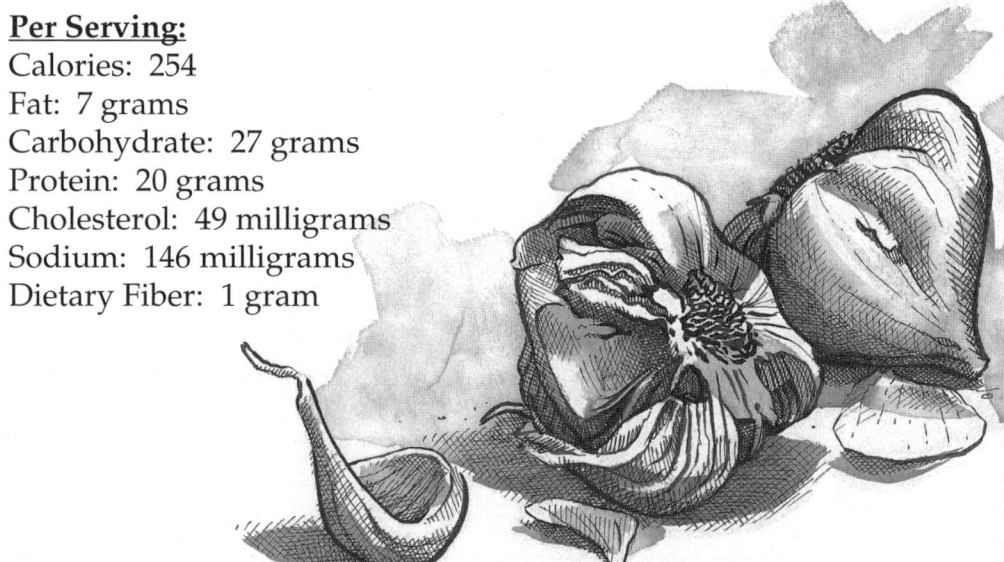

Salmon and Wild Rice Salad

1 (8-ounce) fresh salmon fillet
1/3 cup rice wine vinegar
1/4 cup orange marmalade, all fruit
2 tablespoons low-salt teriyaki or tamari sauce
1 tablespoon grated fresh ginger root
2 teaspoons sesame oil
1 (6-ounce) package wild rice cooked without salt
1 cup fresh snow pea pods
1/2 cup sliced green onions
1/2 cup finely chopped sweet red pepper
Bibb lettuce leaves for garnish

Place salmon in an 8-inch square dish and set aside.

Combine next 5 ingredients in a jar; cover tightly and shake vigorously.

Pour half of mixture over salmon, turning to coat well. Set aside remaining dressing mixture.

Cover salmon and chill 1 hour.

Drain salmon, discarding marinade; then place salmon in a broiler pan.

Broil salmon 5 inches from heat for 3 to 5 minutes on each side or until fish flakes easily when tested with a fork.

Separate salmon into chunks and cool.

Combine salmon, cooked rice, and remaining dressing mixture. Toss gently.

Cover and chill for at least 3 hours. Serve on lettuce leaves.

Yield: 5 servings

Per Serving:
Calories: 323
Carbohydrates: 49 grams
Cholesterol: 31 milligrams
Dietary Fiber: 4 grams
Fat: 7 grams
Protein: 20 grams
Sodium: 389 milligrams

Southwest Marinated Bean Salad

1 can Great Northern beans, rinsed and drained
1 can black beans, rinsed and drained
1 can kidney beans, rinsed and drained
1 can whole kernel corn, rinsed and drained
1 small jar diced pimiento, drained
1 medium carrot, chopped
2 tablespoons olive oil
1/2 cup cider vinegar
2 garlic cloves, crushed
1/2 teaspoon sea salt and pepper
1/8 teaspoon chili pepper

Combine first 6 ingredients in a large bowl. Set aside.
Combine remaining ingredients and pour over bean mixture.
Cover and refrigerate for several hours to allow beans to marinate.
Yield: 6 servings

Per Serving:
Calories: 330
Fat: 6 grams
Carbohydrate: 57 grams
Protein: 17 grams
Cholesterol: 0 milligrams
Sodium: 453 milligrams
Dietary Fiber: 11 grams

Sunshine Spinach Salad

5 cups (packed) spinach leaves, washed and dried
1/2 red onion, thinly sliced
1/2 red pepper, thinly sliced
1 small cucumber, sliced
1 can mandarin oranges, drained (or 2 oranges, peeled and chopped into bite-size pieces)
Low-fat vinaigrette dressing (see recipe under dressings)

Toss all ingredients in a large salad bowl. Add dressing to taste and toss again.
Serve immediately.
Yield: 4 servings

Per Serving:
Calories: 84
Fat: 1 gram
Carbohydrate: 16 grams
Protein: 3 grams
Cholesterol: 0 milligrams
Sodium: 106 milligrams
Dietary Fiber: 5 grams

Sweet Slaw

1 small head green cabbage, cored and finely shredded
3 carrots, shredded
2 stalks celery, thinly sliced
1 teaspoon low-sodium vegetable seasoning
1/3 cup raisins
2 crisp green apples, peeled cored, and sliced
1-2 tablespoons raspberry vinegar
2-3 tablespoons unsweetened apple juice concentrate
1/2 cup nonfat yogurt
Fresh parsley
Thinly sliced red apple

Combine first three ingredients.
Season with vegetable seasoning.
Add raisins and apples.
Combine vinegar, apple juice concentrate, and yogurt. Add to cabbage mixture. Mix well and adjust seasonings to taste.
Place in a serving bowl and garnish with fresh parsley sprigs in the center of the salad with thin apple slices (red skin up) arranged in a spokelike design around the parsley.
Cover and chill several hours so flavors will blend before serving.
Yield: 8 servings

Per Serving:
Calories: 82
Fat: 0 grams
Carbohydrates: 20 grams
Protein: 2 grams
Cholesterol: 0 milligrams
Sodium: 46 milligrams
Dietary Fiber: 5 grams

Tomato-Basil Couscous Salad

1 1/4 cups boiling water
1 1/4 cups whole wheat couscous, uncooked
2 cups chopped tomato
1 cup finely chopped fresh basil
1/3 cup finely chopped purple onion

1/4 cup apple cider vinegar
2 tablespoons olive oil
1/4 teaspoon sea salt
1/4 teaspoon pepper'

Combine boiling water and couscous. Cover and let stand 5 minutes. Uncover and fluff with a fork. Cool.

Combine couscous, tomato, basil, and onion. Set aside.

Combine apple cider vinegar and remaing ingredients in a jar; cover tightly, and shake vigorously. Drizzle over salad and toss gently.

Cover and chill. Toss befoe serving.

Yield: 6 servings

Per Serving:
Calories: 216
Fat: 5 grams
Carbohydrate: 34 grams
Protein: 6 grams
Cholesterol: 0 milligrams
Sodium: 291 milligrams
Dietary Fiber: 2 grams

Tomato-Cucumber Salad With Dill Dressing

1 head leaf lettuce
4 small tomatoes, cut into wedges
1 medium cucumber, scored and sliced
1/2 small purple onion, sliced and separated into rings

Line individual plates with lettuce leaves.
Arrange tomato, cucumber, and onion in pinwheel fashion on plates.
Top with dill dressing.
Yield: 8 servings

Per Serving:
Calories: 21 grams
Fat: 0 grams
Carbohydrate: 5 grams
Protein: 1 gram
Cholesterol: 0 milligrams
Sodium: 7 milligrams
Dietary Fiber: 1 gram

Vegetable Pasta Salad

1 package (8-ounces) medium-sized shell-shaped or spiral pasta
3/4 cup Creamy Italian Dressing, (see recipe)
1 cup small broccoli florets
12 cherry tomatoes, halved
1/2 cup zucchini, cut into 1/4-inch slices then halved
1/2 cup yellow squash, cut into 1/4-inch slices, then halved
1/4 cup green bell pepper, cut into 1-inch squares
1/4 cup yellow bell pepper, cut into 1-inch squares
1/4 cup red bell pepper, cut into 1-inch squares
1/2 cup carrot, sliced diagonally
1/2 cup cauliflower
1/4 cup red onion, chopped

Cook pasta in boiling water according to package directions, omitting salt and oil. Rinse in cold water and drain well. Transfer to a large bowl and add Creamy Italian Dressing. Mix well.
Add remaining vegetables and toss well.
Cover and refrigerate at least 2 hours before serving.
Yield: 8 servings

Per Serving:
Calories: 124
Fat: 2 grams
Carbohydrate: 21 grams
Protein: 4 grams
Cholesterol: 0 milligrams
Sodium: 50 milligrams
Dietary Fiber: 1 gram

CHAPTER SIX
Dressings, Sauces, Spreads, & Dips

" Who satisfies your mouth with good things, so that your youth is renewed like the eagle's. "

(Psalm 103:5)

Apple Butter

This recipe is easy to make as you do other chores around the house.
Also makes great gifts for your friends!

10 large apples, peeled
2 cups unsweetened apple juice
1/2 cup raw honey or brown rice syrup
2 teaspoons cinnamon
1/2-1 teaspoon ground cloves
1/2 teaspoon allspice
Dash of sea salt
1/2 teaspoon vanilla
Juice and grated rind of 1 small lemon

Wash and cut apples into quarters. Place them in large pot and add remaining ingredients.

Cook over medium-low heat until tender.

Cool slightly and puree in blender until smooth.

Pour applesauce back into Dutch oven and cook over low heat for several hours until the sauce turns brown. (Stir <u>often</u> so that the apple butter does not stick to the bottom of the pot.)

Yield: About 1 quart

Per Tablespoon:
Calories: 34
Fat: 0 grams
Carbohydrate: 9 grams
Protein: 0 grams
Cholesterol: 0 milligrams
Sodium: 5 milligrams
Dietary Fiber: 1 gram

Basil Vinaigrette Dressing

1 shallot
2 cloves garlic
1 tablespoon Dijon mustard
1 cup torn, lightly packed
 basil leaves
Salt, fresh-ground pepper
1 tablespoon red wine vinegar

1 tablespoon fresh-squeezed
 lemon juice
4 tablespoons dry white wine
3 tablespoons fat-free
 chicken broth

Combine all ingredients in a blender.
Puree until smooth.
Pour into a lidded jar and chill at least 2 hours.
Yield: 3/4 cup

Per Tablespoon:
Calories: 9
Fat: 0 grams
Carbohydrate: 1 gram
Protein: 0 grams
Cholesterol: 0 milligrams
Sodium: 52 milligrams
Dietary Fiber: 0 grams

* *Another delicious Jane Snow creation.*

* Our thanks to Jane Snow for creating delicious low-fat and fat-free dressings that sparkle with the tang of fresh lemon juice and fresh herbs. So many low-fat dressings have no taste but her dressings taste as good or better than regular-fat commercial dressings.

Black Bean Salsa

2 cans black beans, rinsed and drained
1 can whole kernel corn, drained
2 large tomatoes, seeded and chopped
1 large avocado, peeled and finely chopped
1 small purple onion, finely chopped
1 tablespoon fresh cilantro, chopped
3 tablespoons lime juice
1 tablespoon vinegar
1/2 teaspoon salt
1/4 teaspoon pepper

Combine all ingredients in a large bowl and mix well. Cover and chill.
Garnish fresh cilantro sprigs and fresh tomato slices, if desired. Serve with fat-free tortilla chips.
Yield: 6 cups

Per Serving:
Calories: 279
Fat: 6 grams
Carbohydrate: 45 grams
Protein: 14 grams
Cholesterol: 0 milligrams
Sodium: 292 milligrams
Dietary Fiber: 16 grams

Black Bean Sauce

1 can black beans, rinsed and drained
1/3 cup water
1 teaspoon olive oil
2 tablespoons fat-free chicken broth
3 cloves garlic, minced
1 tablespoon minced cilantro
1/4 cup diced sweet red pepper
Pinch of sea salt
Low-sodium soy or tamari sauce to taste

Puree beans and water in a blender until smooth.
Saute garlic, cilantro, and red pepper in oil and chicken broth over medium heat.
Add bean puree to herbs and pepper and cook for 10 minutes.
Season to taste with salt and tamari sauce.
Yield: 2 cups (6 servings)

Note: Delicious over rice or millet.

Per Serving:
Calories: 93
Fat: 1 gram
Carbohydrate: 16 grams
Protein: 6 grams
Cholesterol: 0 milligrams
Sodium: 205 milligrams
Dietary Fiber: 5 grams

Chickpea Sandwich Spread

1 cup dried chickpeas
6 cups water
3 medium boiling potatoes unpeeled
3 cloves garlic, minced

2 1/2 tablespoons lemon juice
1/4 teaspoon salt
2-3 green onions, finely chopped
Whole wheat pita bread

Soak overnight uncooked chickpeas in large pot with about 6 cups of water. Drain and discard soaking water.

Add 6 cups fresh water to chickpeas and bring to a boil. Simmer for 1 1/2 hours.

Cut potatoes into cubes (about 1-inch) and add to chickpeas. Simmer 30 minutes more or until chickpeas and potatoes are tender. Remove from heat and drain cooking water; reserving 1/4 cup.

Allow chickpeas and potatoes to cool about 10 minutes, then transfer to a food processor or blender.

Add garlic, lemon juice, and salt. Puree until loose and smooth; adding reserved liquid as needed.

Remove from processor and stir in green onions.

Serve with fresh vegetables such as tomatoes, cucumbers, shredded carrot, lettuce, and sprouts in pita pockets.

Yield: 8 servings

Note: Will keep refrigerated up to 5 days.

Per Serving:
Calories: 163
Fat: 2 grams
Carbohydrate: 31 grams
Protein: 8 grams
Cholesterol: 0 milligrams
Sodium: 106 milligrams
Dietary Fiber: 4 grams

Garbanzo-Carrot Vegetable Spread
(This makes a great appetizer when served as a dip or spread for vegetables)

1 (16-ounce) can garbanzo beans
3/4 cup raw shredded carrots
1/8 cup raisins or currants
2 tablespoons parsley flakes

1/4 cup fresh lime juice
1/4 teaspoon sea salt
Sprinkle of paprika
Pimento and green pepper strips for garnish

Combine beans, carrots, and currants in blender. Puree until smooth. (If necessary, add small amounts of water to thin.)

Spoon puree into bowl and add parsley flakes, lime juice, and salt. Sprinkle paprika on top and garnish with pimento and green pepper strips.

Arrange fresh vegetables on serving platter and serve.

Yield: 1 1/4 cups

Per Tablespoon:
Calories: 30
Fat: 0 grams
Carbohydrate: 5 grams
Protein: 2 grams
Cholesterol: 0 milligrams
Sodium: 32 milligrams
Dietary Fiber: 0 grams

Fat-Free Dill Dressing

3/4 cup plain nonfat yogurt
1/4 cup fat-free mayonnaise
1 teaspoon chopped fresh dill
1 teaspoon chopped fresh chives
Sprinkle of pepper

Combine all ingredients and blend well. Chill.
Yield: 1 cup (1 tablespoon = 1 serving)

Per Serving:
Calories: 9
Fat: 0 grams
Carbohydrate: 2 grams
Protein: 1 gram
Cholesterol: 0 milligrams
Sodium: 56 milligrams

Fresh Fruit Dip
(This is one of our children's favorites!)

1 (8-ounce) carton nonfat yogurt
1/4 cup unsweetened applesauce
1 tablespoon brown rice syrup or honey
1/2 teaspoon vanilla
1/8 teaspoon cinnamon
Dash of nutmeg

Combine all ingredients in small bowl mixing well.
Serve with fresh fruit, especially apple slices.
Yield: 1 1/4 cups

Per Tablespoon:
Calories: 5
Fat: 0 grams
Carbohydrate: 1 gram
Protein: 0 grams
Cholesterol: 0 milligrams
Sodium: 6 milligrams
Dietary Fiber: 0 grams

Fresh Vegetable Dip

2 cups yogurt cream cheese
Juice of half a lemon
1 medium cucumber, peeled and finely diced
2 tablespoons fresh dill, chopped
Drop of hot sauce (optional)
Salt and pepper to taste

Combine all ingredients in mixing bowl and mix well. Chill for 1-2 hours to allow flavors to blend.
Serve with fresh vegetables.
Yield: 2 1/4 cups

Per Tablespoon:
Calories: 5
Fat: 0 grams
Carbohydrate: 1 gram
Protein: 1 gram
Cholesterol: 0 milligrams
Sodium: 13 milligrams
Dietary Fiber: 0 grams

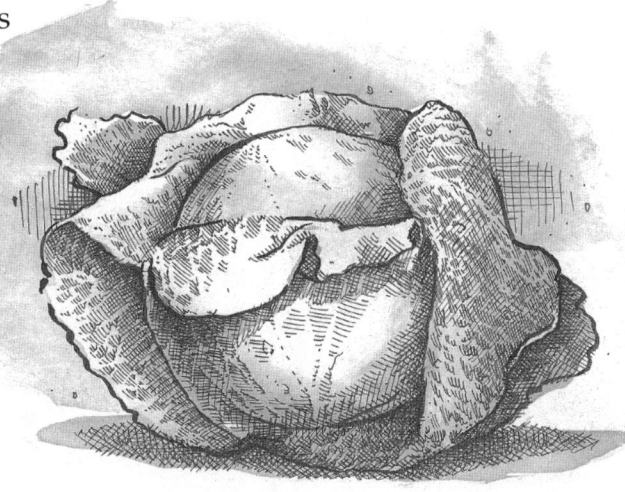

Garlic Bean Dip

1 (15-ounce) can black beans
2 cloves garlic, minced
1 tablespoon fresh cilantro, chopped
Juice of 2 limes
Chili powder and ground cumin to taste

Drain and rinse black beans. Mash thoroughly and blend in next 4 ingredients, adjusting the seasonings to taste.
Yield: 3-4 servings

Per Serving:
Calories: 125
Fat: 0 grams
Carbohydrate: 23 grams
Protein: 8 grams
Cholesterol: 0 milligrams
Sodium: 8 milligrams
Dietary Fiber: 8 grams

Homemade Ketchup

1 large can tomato juice
1/2 cup lemon juice
Dash allspice
1/2 teaspoon paprika
1/2 teaspoon sea salt

1 teaspoon onion powder
1/4 teaspoon garlic powder
2 1/2 tablespoons honey*
1 teaspoon dry mustard
1/2 teaspoon pepper

Combine all ingredients in a saucepan and mix well.
Bring to a boil and simmer uncovered for 2 hours until thick.
Pour into lidded jar and chill.
Yield: about 1 quart

Option: 2 1/2 tablespoons brown rice syrup

Per Tablespoon:
Calories: 7
Fat: 0 grams
Carbohydrate: 2 grams
Protein: 0 grams
Cholesterol: 0 milligrams
Sodium: 96 milligrams
Dietary Fiber: 0 grams

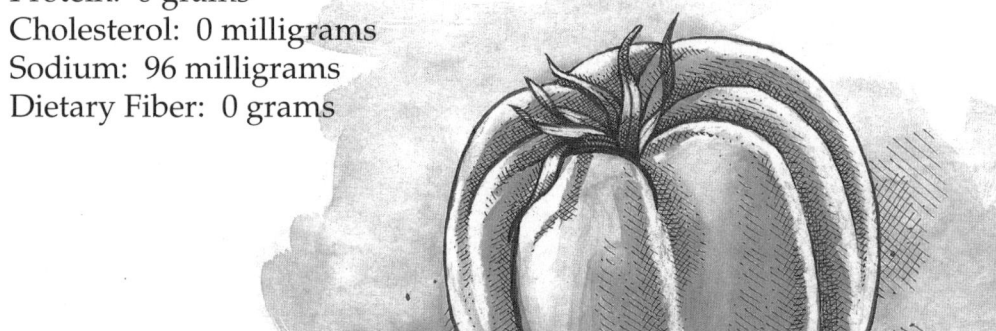

Honey Dijon Dressing

1 shallot
1 clove garlic
3 tablespoons Dijon mustard
Salt, fresh ground pepper
1 tablespoon red wine vinegar
3 tablespoons honey

1 tablespoon fresh-squeezed lemon juice
1/4 cup sweet white wine
1/4 cup fat-free chicken broth
1/2 cup fat-free sour cream

Combine all ingredients except sour cream in a blender.
Puree until smooth.
Pour in a bowl and beat in sour cream with a fork.
Pour in a lidded jar and chill at least 2 hours.
Yield: 1 1/2 cups

<u>Per Tablespoon:</u>
Calories: 19
Fat: 0 grams
Carbohydrate: 3 grams
Protein: 0 grams
Cholesterol: 0 milligrams
Sodium: 41 milligrams
Dietary Fiber: 0 grams

* Another delicious Jane Snow creation.

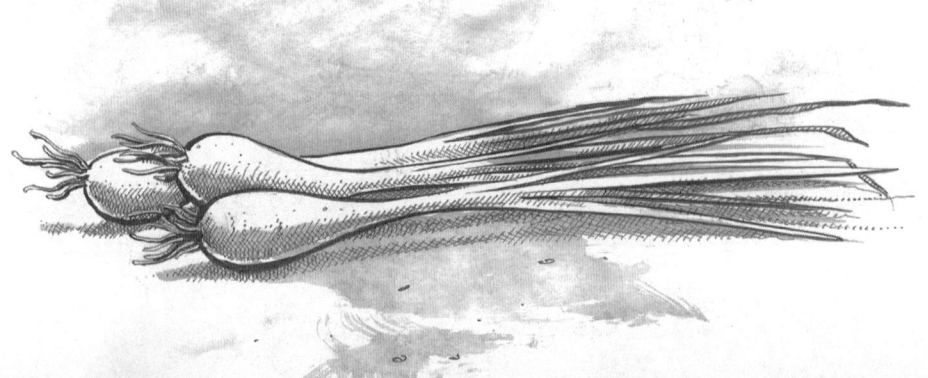

Low-Fat Creamy Italian Dressing

1 shallot
1 clove garlic
1 tablespoon Dijon mustard
Salt, fresh-ground pepper
2 teaspoons Italian seasoning
1 large green onion, chopped
1 tablespoon red wine vinegar
1 tablespoon fresh-squeezed lemon juice
1 tablespoon extra-virgin olive oil
4 tablespoons dry white wine
3 tablespoons chicken broth
1/2 cup fat-free sour cream

Combine all ingredients except sour cream in a blender. Puree until smooth.

Pour into a bowl and beat in sour cream with a fork until smooth.

Pour into a lidded jar. Chill at least 2 hours for flavors to blend.
Yield: 1 1/4 cups

Per Tablespoon:
Calories: 23
Fat: 2 grams
Carbohydrate: 1 gram
Protein: 0 grams
Cholesterol: 0 milligrams
Sodium: 43 milligrams
Dietary Fiber: 0 grams

* Another delicious Jane Snow creation.

Low-Fat Vinaigrette

1 shallot
1 clove garlic
1 tablespoon Dijon mustard
Pinch of sea salt and pepper
1 tablespoon red wine vinegar
1 tablespoon fresh-squeezed lemon juice

1 tablespoon extra-virgin olive oil
4 tablespoons dry white wine
3 tablespoons fat-free chicken broth

Combine all ingredients in a blender.
Puree until smooth and pour into a lidded jar.
Chill at least 2 hours.
Yield: 3/4 cup

Per Tablespoon:
Calories: 16
Fat: 1 gram
Carbohydrate: 0 grams
Protein: 0 grams
Cholesterol: 0 milligrams
Sodium: 46 milligrams
Dietary Fiber: 0 grams

Another delicious Jane Snow creation.

Low-Fat Ranch Dressing

1/2 cup fat-free sour cream
1/2 cup nonfat buttermilk
1 tablespoon real mayonnaise
1 teaspoon fresh-squeezed
   lemon juice

1 tablespoon powdered ranch
   dressing mix

Combine all ingredients and beat with a whisk until smooth.
Refrigerate.
Yield: 1 cup

Per Tablespoon:
Calories: 20
Fat: 0 grams
Cholesterol: 0 milligrams
Sodium: 15 milligrams
Protein: 0 grams
Carbohydrate: 1 gram
Dietary Fiber: 0 grams

* Another delicious Jane Snow creation.

Marinara Sauce

3 tablespoons fat-free vegetable or chicken stock
2 medium onions, chopped
4 garlic cloves, crushed
2 medium carrots, finely chopped
8 medium tomatoes, peeled, seeded, and coarsely chopped
3 tablespoons fresh basil,* coarsely chopped
2 tablespoons fresh oregano,* coarsely chopped
2 tablespoons fresh parsley* coarsely chopped
1/2 teaspoon sea salt

Saute onions, garlic, and carrots in chicken stock for 2 to 3 minutes in large saucepan. Stir in tomatoes, basil, oregano, parsley, and salt.

Cover and simmer over low heat for 20 minutes. Uncover and simmer for 10 minutes.

Cool slightly and pour into a blender or food processor. Process until pureed.

Yield: 5 cups

*Note: Most grocery stores now carry fresh herbs in their fresh vegetables section. If you cannot find fresh herbs, substitute about 1/3 the amount of dried leaf herbs.

Per 4 oz. Serving:
Calories: 38
Fat: 0 grams
Carbohydrate: 8 grams
Protein: 1 gram
Cholesterol: 0 milligrams
Sodium: 158 milligrams
Dietary Fiber: 2 grams

Tomatoes are rich in vitamin C and are a good source of beta carotene and potassium. A medium tomato has about as much fiber as a slice of whole wheat bread!

Orange Pancake and Waffle Syrup
(Try the variation to make other fresh fruit syrups.)

2 cups fresh orange juice
1 tablespoon lemon juice
1/4 cup brown rice syrup or
    raw honey
1 tablespoon cornstarch or
    arrowroot powder
1 tablespoon water

Simmer first 3 ingredients over medium low heat for 5 minutes.
Add cornstarch that has been dissolved in 1 tablespoon water and simmer until thick, stirring constantly, about 3 minutes.
Yield: 2 cups

Variation: Omit the orange juice and substitute 1/2 cup water with honey and lemon juice. Then add 2 cups fresh blueberries or strawberries and simmer 10 minutes before adding cornstarch mixture.

Per Tablespoon :
Calories: 16
Fat: 0 grams
Carbohydrate: 4 grams
Protein: 0 grams
Cholesterol: 0 milligrams
Sodium: 0 milligrams
Dietary Fiber: 0 grams

Orange-Yogurt Fruit Dip

1 (8-ounce) carton nonfat vanilla yogurt
1 1/2 teaspoons frozen orange juice concentrate
1 tablespoon honey or brown rice syrup

Combine all ingredients and mix well. Chill.
Serve with fresh fruit.
Yield: 1 cup

Per Tablespoon:
Calories: 13
Fat: 0 grams
Carbohydrate: 3 grams
Protein: 1 gram
Cholesterol: 0 milligrams
Sodium: 7 milligrams
Dietary Fiber: 0 grams

Quick Pizza Sauce

1 (8-ounce) can no-salt tomato sauce
1/2 teaspoon honey or brown rice syrup
1/2 teaspoon oregano
1/2 teaspoon basil
1 teaspoon Italian seasoning
1/4 teaspoon garlic powder
1/8 teaspoon pepper

Combine all ingredients and cook for 15-20 minutes to allow flavors to blend.
Yield: 1 cup (enough for 2: 15 inch pizzas)

Per 1/2 cup Serving:
Calories: 45
Fat: 0 grams
Carbohydrate: 11 grams
Protein: 2 grams
Cholesterol: 0 milligrams
Sodium: 0 milligrams
Dietary Fiber: 2 grams

Spinach Dip

1 package chopped spinach
1 cup yogurt cream cheese
1/2 cup nonfat sour cream

1/2 cup fresh parsley, minced
3 scallions, chopped
Juice of a half lemon

Thaw frozen package of chopped spinach and squeeze thoroughly to remove excess water.

Combine spinach and remaining ingredients in blender or food processor and process until well blended.

Season to taste with salt and pepper. Chill before serving to allow flavors to blend.

Yield: 2 cups

<u>**Per Tablespoon:**</u>
Calories: 11
Fat: 0 grams
Carbohydrate: 1 gram
Protein: 1 gram
Cholesterol: 0 milligrams
Sodium: 11 milligrams
Dietary Fiber: 0 grams

Yogurt "Cream" Cheese

1 quart chilled plain nonfat yogurt
  (Dannon works well)

Drain yogurt by placing an 18-inch square piece of cheese cloth inside a large mesh strainer. Pour in yogurt and tie edges of cheese cloth together well. (When cheese cloth was not available, I have used a couple of large coffee filters and covered the strainer with a plastic lid. A yogurt funnel may also be used in place of cheese cloth. You can usually find them in gourmet kitchen shops or health food stores.)

Place strainer over a large bowl and set it in your refrigerator. Let it drain for 2 days, checking the bowl and emptying it, as necessary, of the liquid that has drained out. The result will be a "cheese" with the consistency between sour cream and cream cheese.

Use in frostings and spreads.

Yield: Approximately 2 cups

Per Tablespoon:
Calories: 5
Fat: 0 grams
Carbohydrate: 1 gram
Protein: 1 gram
Cholesterol: 0 milligrams
Sodium: 7 milligrams
Dietary Fiber: 0 grams

CHAPTER SEVEN

Vegetable Side Dishes

" And the earth brought forth grass, the herb that yields seed according to its kind, and the tree that yields fruit, whose seed is in itself according to its kind.

And God saw that it was good. "

(Genesis 1:12)

Apple Acorn Squash

2 small acorn squash
2 apples; peeled, cored, and chopped
1/2 cup currants
Apple juice concentrate
Vegetable cooking spray

Cut squash in half. Scoop out the middle so that it can be filled. Place in a glass baking dish that has been lighly sprayed with cooking spray.

Combine apple and currants and fill the middle of each squash half.

Drizzle apple juice concentrate over the top

Bake at 350 degrees for 30-35 minutes or until squash is tender when tested with a fork.

Yield: 4 servings

Per Serving:
Calories: 73
Fat: 0 grams
Carbohydrate: 19 grams
Protein: 1 gram
Cholesterol: 0 milligrams
Sodium: 2 milligrams
Dietary Fiber: 1 gram

Apple Sweet Potatoes

2 medium raw sweet potatoes, peeled and sliced thin
3 medium apples, peeled and sliced thin
2 tablespoons brown rice syrup
Vegetable cooking spray
1 tablespoon unbleached flour
1/4 teaspoon cinnamon
1/4 teaspoon salt
1/2 cup water

Arrange a thin layer of sweet potatoes in a 2 quart casserole dish that has been lightly sprayed with vegetable cooking spray.

Arrange a thin layer of apple slices on top of sweet potatoes and repeat layers.

Combine next 5 ingredients and pour over the layers of sweet potatoes and apples.

Cover and bake at 375 degrees for 50-60 minutes.

Yield: 6 servings

Per Serving:
Calories: 100
Fat: 0 grams
Carbohydrate: 23 grams
Protein: 1 gram
Cholesterol: 0 milligrams
Sodium: 121 milligrams
Dietary Fiber: 3 grams

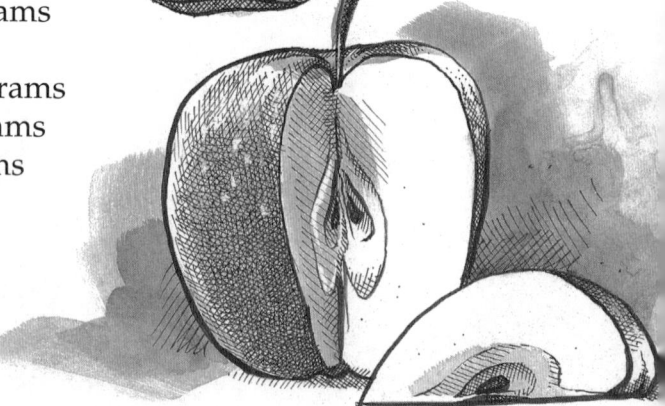

Baked Acorn Squash
With Currant Sauce

1 acorn squash, halved and seeds removed
2 tablespoons currants or raisins
1/2 cup fresh orange juice
1/2 teaspoon cinnamon
Dash nutmeg
Dash sea salt

Spray glass baking dish with vegetable cooking spray. Place acorn squash halves in baking dish and bake at 350 degrees until tender.

Combine remaining ingredients in blender and blend until smooth. Pour into small saucepan and warm over low heat.

Pour currant sauce into hot squash cavity and serve.

Yield: 2 servings

Per Serving:
Calories: 89
Fat: 0 grams
Carbohydrate: 22 grams
Protein: 2 grams
Cholesterol: 0 milligrams
Sodium: 5 milligrams
Dietary Fiber: 0 grams

Baked Potato Croquettes

These baked croquettes make an excellent appetizer for parties or a crunchy accompaniment for roasted or broiled chicken.

4 cups cooked mashed potatoes (mashed with fat-free chicken broth)
1/2 cup egg beaters
2-4 tablespoons fat-free chicken broth
3-4 tablespoons fresh chives, chopped
1/2 teaspoon sea salt
1/8 teaspoon pepper
1 1/2 cups crush fat-free cracker crumbs
1 tablespoon butter, melted
1/4 teaspoon paprika
Vegetable cooking spray

Combine first 6 ingredients; mix well. Divide into 8 equal portions and make into oblong shape. (When making these as an appetizer, divide into smaller portions.)

Roll in cracker crumbs and place on baking sheet that has been lightly sprayed with cooking spray.

Cover and refrigerate for several hours. (At this point, the croquettes may be frozen for later use.)

Combine melted butter and paprika. Drizzle over croquettes.

Bake at 375 degrees for 25 minutes or until golden. Garnish with extra chopped chives. (When baking frozen croquettes, just increase the baking time to 35-40 minutes.)

Yield: 8 servings

Per Serving:
Calories: 233
Carbohydrate: 46 grams
Cholesterol: 1 milligram
Dietary Fiber: 0 grams

Fat: 1 gram
Protein: 10 grams
Sodium: 278 milligrams

CranApple Sweet Potatoes

4 sweet potatoes, peeled and cut into 1-inch cubes
1 large green apple, peeled and diced
1 cup raw cranberries
1/2 cup raisins
2 tablespoons raw honey or brown rice syrup
1/2 cup fresh orange juice
Vegetable cooking spray

Arrange sweet potato chunks in large baking dish.
Top with diced apple, cranberries, and raisins.
Drizzle honey or rice syrup on top and pour orange juice over the entire dish.
Cover and bake about 1 hour or until sweet potatoes are tender.
Yield: 6 servings

Per Serving:
Calories: 265
Fat: 0 grams
Carbohydrate: 65 grams
Protein: 3 grams
Cholesterol: 0 milligrams
Sodium: 16 milligrams
Dietary Fiber: 8 grams

Dilled Asparagus

5-6 fresh asparagus spears, steamed
2 teaspoons fresh dill, snipped
1/2 teaspoon unsalted butter
Juice of 1/2 lemon
Dash of sea salt

Steam asparagus and set aside.
Melt butter in skillet and add lemon juice and fresh dill weed. Add asparagus and toss till coated. Sprinkle with salt if desired.
Yield: 1 serving

Per Serving:
Calories: 32
Fat: 2 grams
Carbohydrate: 5 grams
Protein: 0 grams
Cholesterol: 5 milligrams
Sodium: 1 milligram
Dietary Fiber: 0 grams

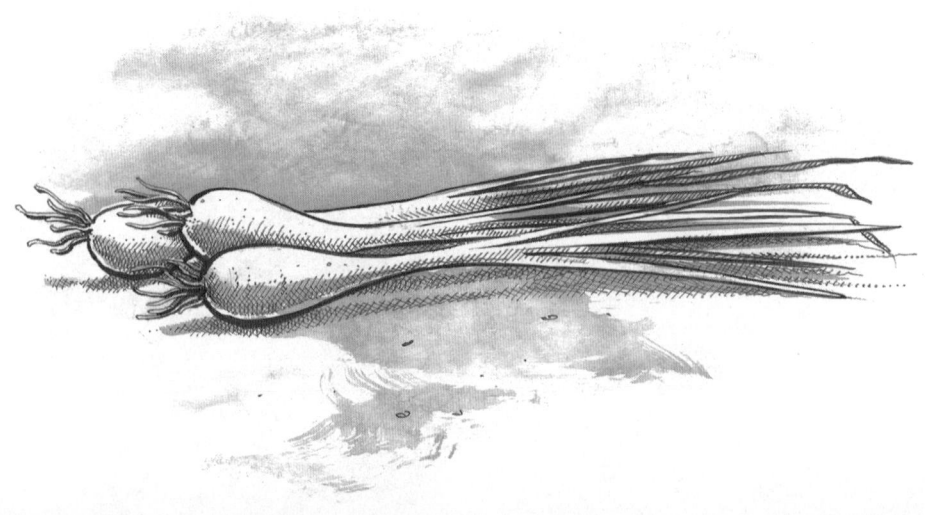

Easy Stir-Fry Squash

3 tablespoons nonfat chicken broth
1 teaspoon reduced sodium soy sauce
2 carrots, thinly sliced
1 yellow or zucchini squash, sliced thin
1 small onion, chopped
1/2 cup egg beaters
2 teaspoons dill weed

Heat chicken broth in a large skillet over medium heat. Add soy sauce and vegetables. Stir-fry until vegetables are tender.

Add egg beaters and dill weed. Stir over heat until egg is scrambled into the vegetable mixture.

Serve immediately.

Yield: 2 servings

Per Serving:
Calories: 97
Fat: 2 grams
Carbohydrate: 10 grams
Protein: 9 grams
Cholesterol: 0 milligrams
Sodium: 306 milligrams
Dietary Fiber: 2 grams

Elegant Eggplant Provencal

1 tablespoon fresh basil,* chopped
1 tablespoon fresh thyme,* chopped
1 tablespoon fresh oregano,* chopped
1 tablespoon fresh rosemary,* chopped
1 small eggplant, peeled and cut into 12 slices
3 small onions, cut into 4 slices each
2 medium tomatoes, peeled and cut into 6 slices each
3 small green peppers, cut into 4 rings each
6 large cloves garlic, minced
2 tablespoons olive oil
Vegetable cooking spray
1/4 cup (1 ounce) grated Parmesan cheese

Combine first 4 herbs; set aside.

Place eggplant slices in large baking dish lightly coated with cooking spray.

Brush each slice with a <u>small</u> amount of olive oil.

Sprinkle each slice with 1/4 teaspoon herb mixture. On top of each eggplant slice, layer onion slices, tomato slices and pepper slices repeating olive oil and sprinkle of herb mixture on top of each layer.

Sprinkle each stack of vegetables with minced garlic, dividing evenly.

Cover and bake for 40 minutes. Uncover and lightly sprinkle each vegetable stack with Parmesan cheese. Bake an additional 5 minutes.

Yield: 12 servings

*1 teaspoon dried basil, thyme, and oregano may be substituted for the fresh herbs. Use only 1/8 teaspoon for each layer.

Per Serving:
Calories: 77
Carbohydrate: 11 grams
Cholesterol: 2 milligrams
Dietary Fiber: 3 grams
Fat: 3 grams
Protein: 3 grams
Sodium: 50 milligrams

Fresh Asparagus and Tomatoes

1 pound fresh asparagus
3 medium tomatoes, sliced thinly
2 tablespoons fresh basil, chopped
1/4 cup part-skim mozzarella cheese, shredded
2 tablespoons apple cider vinegar

Snap off tough ends of asparagus.

Cook asparagus, covered, in a small amount of boiling water for 2 to 3 minutes or until crisp-tender. (You may want to plunge them into ice water to stop the cooking process.) Drain and set aside.

Arrange tomato slices around the outside of a serving plate and sprinkle
with cheese and basil. Drizzle with vinegar.

Arrange asparagus in center of tomato slices.

Yield: 6 servings

Per Serving:
Calories: 65
Fat: 3 grams
Carbohydrate: 4 grams
Protein: 5 grams
Cholesterol: 11 milligrams
Sodium: 94 milligrams
Dietary Fiber: 1 gram

Gala Garlic Potato Mash

6 all-purpose potatoes, peeled and cut into chunks
5-6 cloves garlic, minced
1 teaspoon salt
Garnish with fresh parsley and red pepper strips or paprika

1/2-3/4 cup nonfat chicken broth
1-2 tablespoons nonfat sour cream, (Land O Lakes is good)

Combine first 3 ingredients in large saucepan and cover with cold water. Bring to a boil. Cover, reduce heat, and simmer over medium heat until potatoes are tender. Drain potatoes and return to warm pan.

Mash potatoes with a potato masher or electric mixer. Add chicken broth gradually to make creamy.

Add sour cream and blend well.

Spoon into serving bowl and arrange red pepper strips on top and place parsley in center.

Yield: 6 servings

Per Serving:
Calories: 190
Fat: 0 grams
Carbohydrate: 42 grams
Protein: 5 grams
Cholesterol: 0 milligrams
Sodium: 503 milligrams
Dietary Fiber: 4 grams

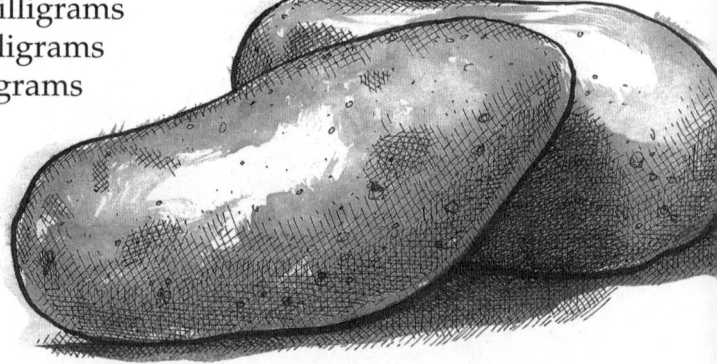

Grecian Green Beans

2 teaspoons olive oil
1 medium onion, thinly sliced
1/4 teaspoon cinnamon
1 1/2 pounds fresh green beans
1/2 cup fat-free chicken broth
1/2 teaspoon sea salt
1/4 teaspoon pepper
1 medium tomato, chopped

Combine olive oil, onion, and cinnamon in large saucepan. Cook until onion is tender.
Add green beans, chicken broth, salt, and pepper.
Bring to a boil. Cover and reduce heat. Simmer, stirring occasionally, for 10 minutes.
Add chopped tomato and cook an additional 2 minutes.
Yield: 6 servings

Per Serving:
Calories: 53
Fat: 2 grams
Carbohydrate: 9 grams
Protein: 2 grams
Cholesterol: 0 milligrams
Sodium: 323 milligrams
Dietary Fiber: 2 grams

Green Bean Bundles

2 pounds fresh green beans
4 cups water
2 small red peppers
1 teaspoon butter
2 teaspoons lemon juice

2 tablespoons sliced green onions
1 tablespoon parsley
8 almonds, coarsely chopped (optional)

Wash beans, trim ends, and remove strings.

Bring water to a boil and add green beans. Cook uncovered about 4-5 minutes until crisp-tender. (You do not want the beans to lose their bright green color.) Drain beans and plunge into cold water to keep them from further cooking. Drain.

Saute onions and parsley in butter and lemon juice for 1-2 minutes. Add green beans and toss.

Divide beans into 8 bundles. Slice peppers into 8 (1/4-inch) rings. Secure each bundle with a pepper slice by slipping it through the center of that pepper slice. Place on a baking sheet. Spoon pan drippings evently over green bean bundles.

Sprinkle chopped almonds on top of each bundle, dividing evenly.

Bake at 350 degrees for 10 minutes or until beans are hot.
Yield: 8 servings

Per Serving:
Calories: 65
Fat: 2 grams
Carbohydrate: 10 grams
Protein: 3 grams
Cholesterol: 1 milligram
Sodium: 23 milligrams
Dietary Fiber: 5 grams

Green Beans with Pimento Strips

1 pound fresh green beans
1 jar pimento, (drained and pimentos cut into strips)

Steam green beans until crisp-tender. Drain.
Arrange green beans in bundles on a serving tray. Place a pimiento strip around the center of each bundle and serve.
Yield: 6 servings

Per Serving:
Calories: 24
Fat: 0 grams
Carbohydrate: 5 grams
Protein: 1 gram
Cholesterol: 0 milligrams
Sodium: 5 milligrams
Dietary Fiber: 3 grams

Grilled Vegetables

2 large yellow squash,
   cut into 3/4-inch slices
1 large zucchini,
   cut into 3/4-inch slices
1 large green pepper,
   cut into 1-inch squares

1 large sweet yellow pepper,
   cut into 1-inch squares
1 large sweet red pepper,
   cut into 1-inch squares

Combine vegetables and cook in boiling water to cover 1 to 2 minutes.

Drain vegetables and plunge into cold water to stop the cooking process.

Cook, covered with grilled lid, over medium-hot coals 10 minutes or until tender, turning once.

Yield: 6 servings

Per Serving:
Calories: 34
Fat: 0 grams
Carbohydrate: 8 grams
Protein: 1 gram
Cholesterol: 0 milligrams
Sodium: 3 milligrams
Dietary Fiber: 1 gram

Lighter Potato Latkes

5 large (Idaho) potatoes, peeled
1 medium onion, chopped fine (about 3/4 cup)
1/4 cup egg beaters
1/2 teaspoon Rumford aluminum-free baking powder
1 teaspoon salt
1/4 teaspoon pepper
Vegetable cooking spray
1 egg white, lightly beaten
3 tablespoons all-purpose flour

Grate potatoes and onion using a food processor or the large holes of a hand grater.

Transfer to a colander and squeeze mixture to press out as much liquid as possible.

Combine next 6 ingredients with potatoes and onions in large mixing bowl.

Spray 2 baking sheets with vegetable cooking spray and drop rounded tablespoons of the potato mixture onto the baking sheets. Press lightly with the back of spoon to form a pancake shape. *

Bake in 400 degree oven for 10 minutes or until golden brown. Turn latkes over and bake for about 10 minutes longer until golden brown.

Yield: 2 dozen

*__Variations:__ Bake in a nonstick muffin pan. Fill each muffin cup with 1/3 cup of potato mixture and bake at 400 degrees for 20 minutes. Lower heat to 350 degrees and continue baking until lightly browned (about 20 minutes).

Spinach Latkes: Reduce recipe to 2 medium potatoes. Add to mixture 1/2 pound fresh spinach that has been steamed, chopped and drained and 3 tablespoons fresh chopped dill.

Per Latke:
Calories: 105
Carbohydrate: 21 grams
Cholesterol: 0 milligrams
Dietary Fiber: 0 grams
Fat: 0 grams
Protein: 5 grams
Sodium: 243 milligrams

Potato Gratin

1 large onion, sliced
1 large red pepper, seeded and sliced
1 pound tomatoes, peeled, seeded, and chopped
3 tablespoons fat-free chicken broth
2 cloves garlic, minced
2 tablespoons fresh basil, chopped
2 pounds baking potatoes
1 tablespoon olive oil
1 tablespoon grated Parmesan cheese

Saute onion in a large skillet in chicken broth until soft, about 3-5 minutes.

Add red pepper and saute 3 minutes more, adding more chicken broth if needed.

Add tomatoes and cook until most moisture evaporates. Add garlic and cook 1 minute. Add chopped basil and set aside.

Wash potatoes and slice into 1/4" slices. Spread half of potatoes on the bottom of a 3-quart baking dish that has been lightly sprayed with cooking spray.

Top with half of the vegatables. Repeat layers.

Drizzle with olive oil and cover tightly.

Bake at 400 degrees for 30 minutes. Uncover and sprinkle with 1 tablespoon Parmesan cheese, if desired. Bake another 15 minutes until potatoes are tender and browned. Garnish with 2 tablespoons fresh chopped basil and serve.

Yield: 6 servings

Per Serving:
Calories: 148
Carbohydrate: 27 grams
Cholesterol: 0 milligrams
Dietary Fiber: 2 grams
Fat: 3 grams
Protein: 6 grams
Sodium: 64 milligrams

Sauteed Spinach and Garlic

2 1/2 pounds spinach
pinch of sea salt
1 teaspoon olive oil
2 tablespoons fat-free chicken broth
2 cloves garlic, minced

Discard stems from spinach and wash leaves thoroughly.
Place spinach (with water that is clinging to the leaves) in a large saucepan with a pinch of sea salt.
Cover and cook over medium-high heat for 5 minutes or until just wilted.
Drain thoroughly.
Combine oil, chicken broth, and garlic in a skillet and sautee garlic until tender and fragrant.
Add spinach and cook until most of the liquid evaporates. Serve.
Yield: 4 servings

Per Serving:
Calories: 39
Fat: 1 gram
Carbohydrate: 5 grams
Protein: 3 grams
Cholesterol: 0 milligrams
Sodium: 161 milligrams
Dietary Fiber: 2 grams

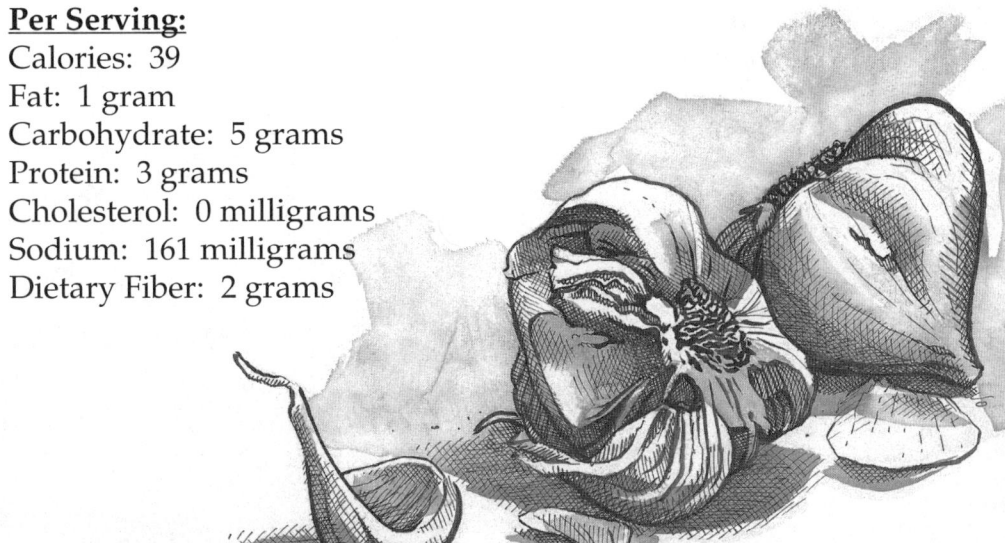

Sauteed Zucchini and Carrots

6 carrots, thinly sliced diagonally
2 teaspoons olive oil
2 ablespoons fat-free chicken broth
1 small onion, thinly sliced
2 medium zucchini, sliced diagonally
3 tablespoons chopped fresh basil
1/2 teaspoon sea salt
1/4 teaspoon pepper

Cook carrots in olive oil over medium-high heat until crisp-tender, about 4 minutes. Stir constantly.

Add onion and cook, stirring constantly, 1 minute.

Add zucchini and remaining ingredients. Cook, stirring constantly, 1 minute.

Serve immediately.

Yield: 6 servings

Per Serving:
Calories: 47
Fat: 2 grams
Carbohydrate: 8 grams
Protein: 1 gram
Cholesterol: 0 milligrams
Sodium: 231 milligrams
Dietary Fiber: 2 grams

Southern Corn Pudding in Tomato Cups

4 medium tomatoes
1/2 cup egg beaters
1 teaspoon honey
1/4 teaspoon sea salt
1/8 teaspoon pepper
1 (8-ounce) can whole kernel corn, well drained
1 teaspoon minced onion
1/3 cup skim milk or evaporated skim milk
1/4 cup shredded Parmesan cheese
Chopped parsley

Preheat oven to 325 degrees.

Cut off a slice about 1/2-inch thick across top of each tomato. Scoop out and discard seeds and pulp, being careful not to tear the tomato shell. Turn upside down to drain over paper towels.

Beat egg beaters, honey, salt, and pepper in medium-sized bowl. Stir in corn, onion, and milk.

Place each tomato, cut side up, in a 6-ounce glass baking cup. Fill each tomato shell with corn mixture.

Bake 45 to 55 minutes or until a knife inserted off-center in filling comes out clean.

Top each tomato with Parmesan cheese and chopped parsley while hot.

Yield: 4 servings.

Per Serving:
Calories: 120
Fat: 3 grams
Carbohydrates: 17 grams
Protein: 9 grams
Cholesterol: 4 milligrams
Sodium: 440 milligrams
Dietary Fiber: 2 grams

Spiked Potatoes

4 large potatoes, unpeeled and cut into large chunks
1 tablespoon of olive oil
1 1/2 tablespoons of salt-free <u>Spike</u>* seasoning
Vegetable cooking spray

Spray a large glass baking dish with cooking spray.
Arrange potatoes in baking dish and drizzle with olive oil.
Sprinkle Spike over potatoes and lightly toss.
Bake at 350 degrees for 1 hour.
Yield: 4 servings

*Spike can be found in most health food stores or larger supermarkets with health food sections.

Variations: Along with potatoes, add 3 carrots, diagonally sliced, and 1 medium onion, cut into chunks.

Per Serving:
Calories: 87
Fat: 3 grams
Carbohydrate: 13 grams
Protein: 1 gram
Cholesterol: 0 milligrams
Sodium: 3 milligrams
Dietary Fiber: 1 gram

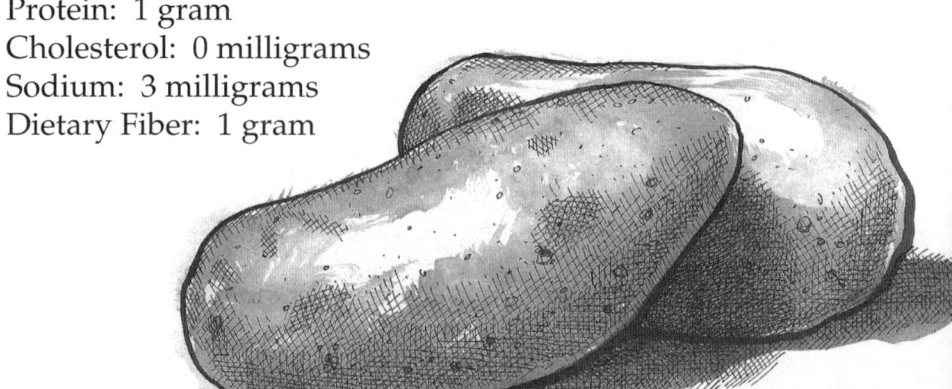

Squash and Onions

1 teaspoon olive oil
2 yellow squash, sliced
1 medium onion, sliced
1/4 teaspoon oregano

1/4 cup water or nonfat chicken broth
1/2 teaspoon reduced-salt soy sauce

Heat oil and soy sauce in medium saucepan and add onions. Saute until transparent.

Add squash and oregano and saute until squash are tender; adding water or chicken broth as needed. Squash should be tender-crisp.

Yield: 2 servings

Per Serving:
Calories: 53
Fat: 2 grams
Carbohydrate: 7 grams
Protein: 2 grams
Cholesterol: 0 milligrams
Sodium: 54 milligrams
Dietary Fiber: 2 grams

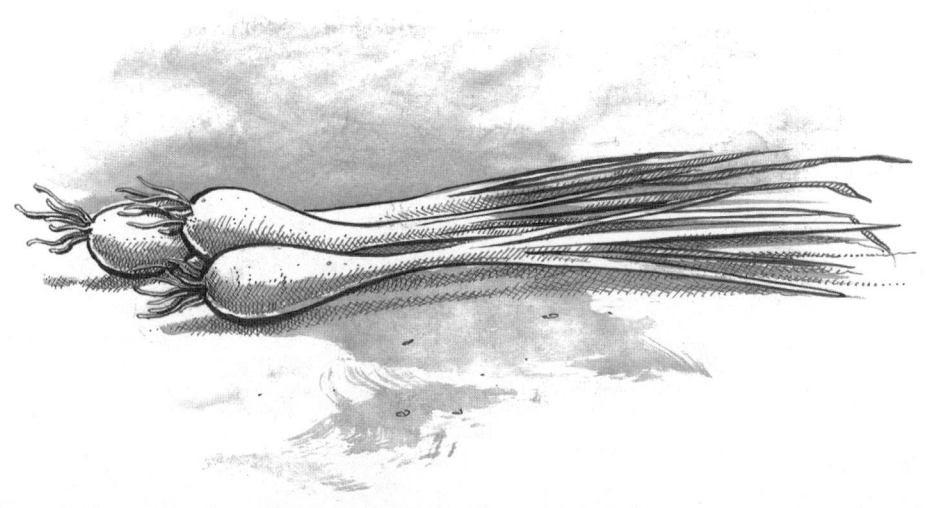

Steamed Cauliflower, Carrots, and Broccoli With Herb Sauce

1 small cauliflower, trimmed into florets
3 large carrots, sliced diagonally
1 small bunch of broccoli, trimmed into florets
1 1/2 cups fat-free chicken broth
1/4 teaspoon dried thyme
1 small piece bay leaf
1 large clove garlic, minced
1/2 teaspoon lemon juice

Steam cauliflower, carrots, and broccoli in vegetable steamer over boiling water until crisp-tender. Transfer to a serving dish and keep warm.

Combine broth and next 4 ingredients in small saucepan. Bring to a boil and reduce volume by half.

Add lemon juice and pour over vegetables.

Yield: 6 servings

Per Serving:
Calories: 21
Fat: 0 grams
Carbohydrate: 4 grams
Protein: 1 gram
Cholesterol: 0 milligrams
Sodium: 214 milligrams
Dietary Fiber: 1 gram

Steamed Garlic Broccoli

1/4 bunch broccoli florets
1 clove garlic, minced
1/2 cup water
Sea salt to taste

Wash broccoli florets and place in a 1 1/2 quart saucepan with water and garlic.
Bring to a boil and reduce heat. Cover and simmer on low for 4 minutes.
Yield: 1 serving

Per Serving:
Calories: 17
Fat: 0 grams
Carbohydrate: 3 grams
Protein: 2 grams
Cholesterol: 0 milligrams
Sodium: 12 milligrams
Dietary Fiber: 0 grams

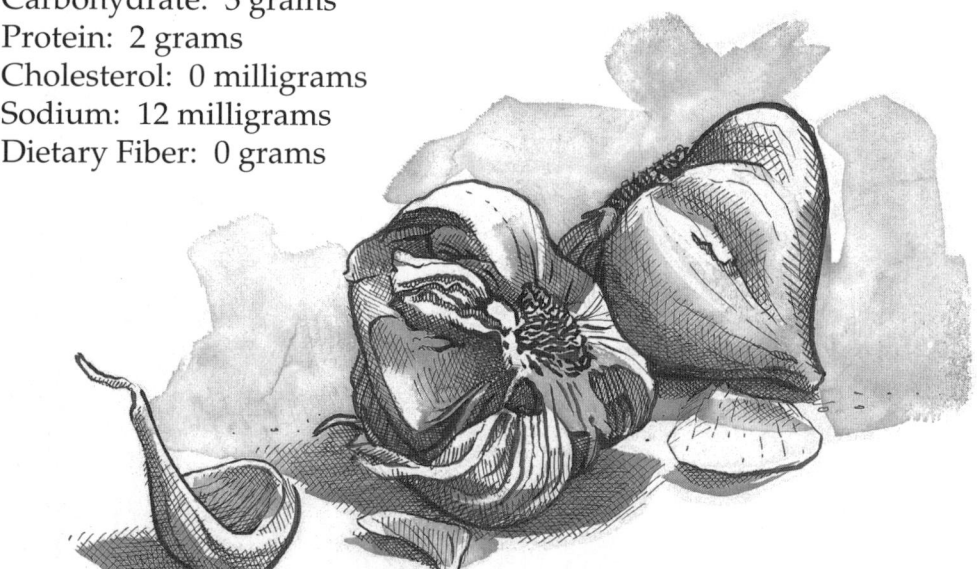

Stuffed Baked Sweet Potatoes

6 medium-sized sweet potatoes
Vegetable cooking spray
1 (6-ounce) can frozen orange
   juice concentrate, thawed and
   undiluted
1 cup crushed pineapple, drained
4 tablespoons chopped pecans

Wash potatoes and spray lightly with cooking spray. Place on baking sheet and bake at 400 degrees for 1 hour or until done.

Split potatoes in half lengthwise. Carefully scoop out pulp, leaving shells intact.

Mash sweet potato pulp and add orange juice concentrate and pineapple. Mix well.

Stuff potato shells with pulp mixture and sprinkle with pecans.

Place stuffed potato shells on a baking sheet and bake at 400 degrees until pecans are lightly toasted and potato is warmed, about 5-10 minutes.

Yield: 6 servings

Per Serving:
Calories: 258
Fat: 3 grams
Carbohydrate: 56 grams
Protein: 2 grams
Cholesterol: 0 milligrams
Sodium: 31 milligrams
Dietary Fiber: 4 grams

Sweet Carrots

6 medium carrots, scraped and sliced diagonally
3/4-1 cup orange juice
1 teaspoon honey

Combine all ingredients in saucepan and bring to a boil. Cover, reduce heat to low, and simmer until carrots are tender.
Yield: 4 servings

Per Serving:
Calories: 69
Fat: 0 grams
Carbohydrate: 16 grams
Protein: 1 gram
Cholesterol: 0 milligrams
Sodium: 30 milligrams
Dietary Fiber: 3 grams

Sweet Sauteed Sugar Snaps

1 pound sugar snap peas
18 pearl onions, peeled
2 tablespoons fat-free chicken broth
1 tablespoon fresh mint leaves
1/2 cup water
12 raw almonds (optional)

Wash pea pods and remove ends and strings.

Saute onions in chicken broth in large saucepan until tender.

Add peas, mint, and water and bring to a boil. Cover, reduce heat, and simmer 5-8 minutes or until tender-crisp.

Remove from heat. Place in warm serving dish, add almonds and serve immediately.

Yield: 6 servings

Per Serving:
Calories: 39
Fat: 1 gram
Carbohydrate: 5 grams
Protein: 2 grams
Cholesterol: 0 milligrams
Sodium: 29 milligrams
Dietary Fiber: 2 grams

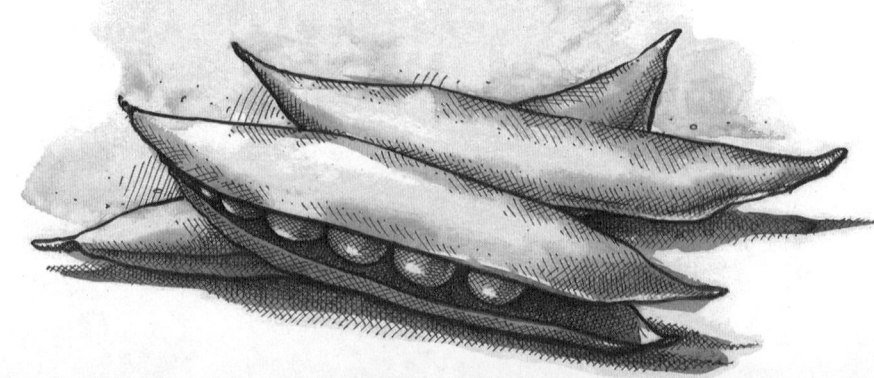

Vegetable Medley

1/2 cup water
1 teaspoon olive oil
1/2 teaspoon salt
1/4 teaspoon pepper
2 cloves garlic, minced
3 medium carrots,
    1/4" diagonal slices
1 large onion, cut in wedges
Fresh chives

1 medium green pepper,
    1/2-inch pieces
1 medium red pepper,
    1/2-inch pieces
2 medium yellow squash,
    1/4" diagonal slices
2 medium zucchini,
    1/4" diagonal slices

Combine first 5 ingredients in Dutch oven and bring to a boil.
Add carrots; cover, reduce heat, and simmer for 5 minutes.
Add onion, peppers, squash, and zucchini. Cover.
Simmer 3 to 4 minutes.
Drain vegetables and place in serving dish.
Sprinkle with fresh chives and serve immediately.
Yield: 8 servings

Per Serving:
Calories: 54
Fat: 1 gram
Carbohydrate: 11 grams
Protein: 2 grams
Cholesterol: 0 milligrams
Sodium: 160 milligrams
Dietary Fiber: 3 grams

Zucchini Fans

6 small zucchini (1 1/4 pounds)
18-20 small tomato slices (1/4-inch thick)
Olive oil-flavored vegetable cooking spray
1/2 teaspoon dried basil leaves
1/4 teaspoon pepper

Wash and cut each zucchini into 4 lengthwise slices, leaving the slices attached at the stem end.

Fan slices out and place a tomato slice in a staggered pattern between each slice.

Place in a 13x9x2 glass baking dish that has been coated with cooking spray. Spray each zucchini fan lightly with cooking spray and sprinkle with basil and pepper.

Cover and bake at 350 degrees for 20 minutes.

Yield: 6 servings

Per Serving:
Calories: 35
Fat: 0 grams
Carbohydrate: 8 grams
Protein: 2 grams
Cholesterol: 0 milligrams
Sodium: 12 milligrams
Dietary Fiber: 2 grams

Zucchini-Tomato Bake

6 medium-sized zucchini, thinly sliced
1/4 cup thinly sliced onion
1 tablespoon olive oil
2 tablespoons chopped fresh parsley
2 ripe tomatoes, sliced
Sea salt and pepper to taste
1 tablespoon Parmesan cheese
Vegetable cooking spray

Steam zucchini and drain. Set aside.

Saute onion in olive oil until tender. Add chopped parsley and stir to heat. Remove from heat and set aside.

Spray an 8x8 glass baking dish with cooking spray.

Arrange a layer of zucchini on bottom of dish, then a layer of sliced tomatoes, then onion mixture. Repeat layers.

Sprinkle with sea salt and pepper and 1 tablespoon Parmesan cheese.

Bake at 350 degrees for 30 minutes.

Yield: 6 servings

Per Serving:
Calories: 45
Fat: 3 grams
Carbohydrate: 5 grams
Protein: 3 grams
Cholesterol: 0 milligrams
Sodium: 22 milligrams
Dietary Fiber: 1 gram

CHAPTER EIGHT

Grain Side Dishes

"...brought beds and basins, earthen vessels and wheat, barley and flour, parched grain and beans, lentils and parched seeds,...For they said 'The people are hungry and weary and thirsty in the wilderness.'"

(2 Samuel 17:28-29)

GRAINS
God's Miracle Food

Whole grains are the foundation of the Genesis Way of life. They provide the finest complex carbohydrates and fiber available in the entire food chain. Grains build muscle, increase energy, and fire up your metabolism. They keep you lean and healthy. Slowly digesting whole grains are **God's natural sugar.** They provide you with a continuous stream of energy. Whole grains are an ideal source of fuel for the brain, nervous system, muscles, hormones, glands, and organs.

A kernel of grain is made up of three parts: the **bran**, the **endosperm**, and the **germ**. The **bran** is the outermost part of the grain and the finest source of fiber. The **endosperm** is primarily starch. As it slowly digests, it produces energy in the form of glucose or sugar. The **germ** is rich in protein and polyunsaturated fatty acids. Gluten, contained in most grains, is a sticky, tough, protein that forms mucus and coats the villi of the intestines. (See Grain Chart)

In the biblical account of Joseph in Egypt, you may recall that Joseph stored grain in order to help the people through the seven years of famine! The Scriptures have more references to grains than to any other food! Here are the grains we have chosen to include in this cookbook. You will enjoy learning to prepare these delicious grain recipes.

MAKE-UP OF A KERNEL OF GRAIN
Oats, brown rice, millet, barley, buckwheat, rye, cornmeal.

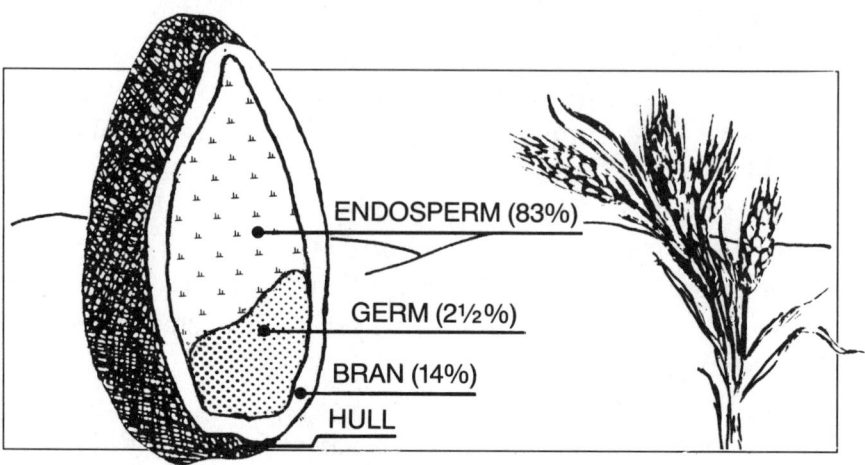

- ENDOSPERM (83%)
- GERM (2½%)
- BRAN (14%)
- HULL

TOTAL NUTRIENTS IN A KERNEL OF GRAIN

GERM	BRAN	ENDOSPERM
Thiamine (B^1)	Pyridoxine (B^6)	Starch
Riboflavin (B^2)	Pantothenic Acid (B^5)	Traces of Vitamins
Pyridoxine (B^6)	Riboflavin (B^2)	& Minerals
Protein	Thiamine (B^1)	
Pantothenic Acid (B^5)	Protein	
Niacin (B^3)		
Vitamin E		

MINERALS

Calcium	Sulphur	Barium
Iron	Iodine	Silver
Phosphorus	Fluorine	Inositol
Magnesium	Chlorine	Folic Acid
Potassium	Sodium	Choline
Manganese	Silicon	And other trace
Copper	Boron	materials

Source: Nutrition Almanac

GRAIN SIDE DISHES

Barley
Barley is mentioned frequently in the Bible and the prophets ate it as their staple food. Barley is a hearty, filling grain. It makes a delicious addition in soups and stews. It can be substituted for rice in most recipes. Barley flour may be used in breads and pancake mixes. It is an excellent source of complete protein, natural sugars and the essential amino acids. Barley is gluten-free and is rich in calcium, iron, thiamin(B1), riboflavin(B2), and niacin(B3).

Buckwheat
Buckwheat can be made into flour for pancakes or eaten as a nutritious, gluten-free cereal. Buckwheat contains complete protein, vitamins, and minerals, especially manganese and magnesium. It is high in rutin, a bioflavinoid, found to be helpful in lowering blood pressure, aiding the circulatory system and easing painful hemorrhoids. The Jewish people eat a traditional buckwheat dish known as Kasha.

Corn
Corn is very economical since it yields three times as much harvest per acre as wheat (Genesis 27:28,KJ). Corn is a high protein seed that is actually a grass! Yellow corn is preferred because of its abundant amount of Vitamin A. It also contains the largest amount of energy producing starch. Its germ is particularly rich in unsaturated fatty acids.

Millet
Millet has the ability to support human life in the absence of all other foods. This makes it unique among the grains. Millet has all the essential amino acids comparable to meat or dairy. It contains all the minerals and is particularly rich in calcium, magnesium, potassium, iron and florine. It is also rich in Vitamins A, B, and C. Millet contains choline, which helps to keep cholesterol levels low! Since millet is an alkaline food, unlike most grains, it is well tolerated by individuals with over-acid and ulcerative conditions. It can be substituted for rice in any recipe. Ezekiel made his famous bread, according to the Lord's recipe (Ezekiel 4:9), using millet.

Oats

Oats are a good source of B vitamins, protein, calcium and iodine. The iodine content of oats is helpful for a slow-working thyroid. Of all the grains, oats are the most acidic and contain a high amount of gluten. The bran of oats is an excellent source of fiber that is beneficial in relieving constipation and removing excess cholesterol. People, as well as horses, will develop endurance and strength by eating oats regularly!

Quinoa

Quinoa is pronounced "keenwah" and is considered by the Academy of Science to contain " the best source of protein in the vegetable kingdom". It is a member of the same family as spinach, beets, chard, and lamb's quarter. Quinoa is high in B vitamins, iron, fiber, calcium and phosphorous. It cooks like rice.

Rice

Rice is the staple food crop for over half the world's population. The average Oriental eats four hundred pounds of rice a year while Americans eat less than ten pounds a year! Unprocessed rice is naturally brown and highly nutritious. There are two major varieties, short and long grain. Brown rice contains ten percent (10%) protein, seven percent (7%) fat, and eighty-three percent (83%) carbohydrates. Rice flour can be added to bread recipes in place of wheat flour. Rice can also be added to soups and stews or eaten as a side dish. Basmati brown rice is a nutty, non-gummy rice that can be purchased at supermarkets and health food stores. Incredibly, there are 7,000 varieties of rice!

Rye

Rye is the heartiest of all the grains. It is high in protein, low in gluten and possesses a strong flavor. Rye has the highest quantity of the amino acid, lysine. This hearty grain can be ground into flour to produce rye or pumpernickel breads. Rye can be used in place of rice or it can be flaked like oats, which makes it easier to cook.

Spelt

Spelt is an ancient grain mentioned in the Bible (Ezekiel 4:9). Allergic individuals tolerate spelt well because of its digestibility. It contains more Vitamin B1 and B2 than any other grain. Spelt is an excellent source of valuable minerals and contains all the essential amino acids. It aids digestion, promotes elimination, and helps the immune system. Spelt flour can be used in recipes calling for whole wheat flour.

Wheat

Wheat is the most widely cultivated grain crop in the world. This popular grain is high in protein, essential minerals, B-vitamins, and vitamin E. Hard wheat has a very high gluten content which helps make bread rise. Soft wheat has less gluten and is more suitable in baking cakes, pie crusts, muffins, and biscuits. Wheat can cause constipation, allergies, bloating and even weight gain. Alternating whole wheat with other grain choices will reduce these problems.

COOKING WHOLE GRAINS

Whole grains can be cooked in a stainless steel or glass pan on the stove. Aluminum pans are not recommended since the softness of aluminum makes it come off in the water during boiling and aluminum may contribute to Alzheimer's disease.

1) Grains must be thoroughly washed before cooking. Use a wire mesh strainer to rinse measured grain.

2) For every cup (8 oz,) of dry grain you cook, use 2.5 cups of water (distilled or spring water), **unless otherwise specified in chart below.**

3) In your pan add the measured amount of water and the washed grain. Cover pan with tight fitting lid and bring to a boil. Reduce the heat to low and cook until all the liquid is absorbed.

4) When done, remove from heat and let stand 5-10 minutes. Fluff with a fork and serve or add to a recipe.

Cooking Times & Proportion for Grains

Grain (1 cup dry)	Water	Cooking Time	Yield
Barley (whole)	3 cups	1 hour 15 minutes	3 1/2 cups
Brown rice	2 cups	1 hour	3 cups
Buckwheat (kasha)	2 cups	15 minutes	2 1/2 cups
Bulgur wheat	2 cups	15-20 minutes	2 1/2 cups
Cracked wheat	2 cups	25 minutes	2 1/3 cups
Millet	3 cups	45 minutes	3 1/2 cups
Coarse cornmeal	4 cups	25 minutes	3 cups
Wild rice	3 cups	1 hour or more	4 cups
Whole wheat berries	3 cups	2 hours	2 2/3 cups
Quinoa	2 cups	15 minutes	2 1/2 cups

Cooking with an electric cooker

If you are using an electric rice cooker, follow the manufacturer's instructions. When purchasing a rice cooker, make certain the cooking pot has a non-stick teflon coating and not an aluminum pot. This will ensure easy cooking and avoid the dangers associated with non-coated aluminum pans.

Grains are God's Best

The Genesis Way is God's best for man's nutritional welfare and grains are at the top of His list. Whole grains keep your tummy full, bowels eliminating, energy high and blood sugar staple. If that doesn't get you excited, remember this fact: Whole grains are low in fat! God's Holy Days (Leviticus 23) are based on the harvesting of these grains and also used in the Tabernacle and Temple offerings outlined in the Scriptures. They are unequaled as a treasure chest of vitality and long-lasting energy. Grains were a staple of the great prophets of the Bible. The prophet, Ezekiel, was told by the Spirit of God (Ezekiel 2:2-3, 4:9) to take wheat, barley, beans, lentils, millet and spelt(form of rye) and make bread from them. Daniel, another great prophet, central to many of the "last day" prophesies, refused to defile himself by eating the king of Babylon's delicacies (Daniel 1:8-16). Instead, eating only a vegetarian diet and pure water, Daniel, looked healthier than any of the other young Israelite men. This cookbook will help you prepare these wholesome grains so that you may be strong and healthy like the prophets of old. Grains are so nutritious that they can sustain us in the absence of other foods.

> Grains are survival foods for the last days! Remember Joseph in Egypt, what did he store up for the famine (Genesis 41:48-49)? Those amazing grains!

Almond Wild and Brown Rice

1/4 cup wild rice
3/4 cup brown rice
1 cup chopped onion
2 tablespoons slivered almonds
1 tablespoon olive oil
2 1/2 cups fat-free chicken broth

> **Saute** rice, onion, and almonds in oil for 5 minutes.
> **Stir** in chicken broth and pour in casserole dish.
> **Cover** and bake at 350 degrees for 1 hour and 15 minutes.
> **Yield:** 6 servings

Per Serving:
Calories: 151
Fat: 4 grams
Carbohydrate: 26 grams
Protein: 4 grams
Cholesterol: 0 milligrams
Sodium: 643 milligrams
Dietary Fiber: 2 grams

Barley Casserole

1 cup barley
4 cups fat-free chicken broth
1 carrot, sliced
1 small leek (white part only), sliced
1 small onion, chopped
1/2 teaspoon thyme, crushed
1/2 teaspoon low-sodium vegetable seasoning (optional)
Chopped fresh parsley for garnish
2-ounce jar pimento

Combine all ingredients, except parsley and pimento in a 2-quart casserole.

Cover and bake in a preheated 350 degree oven for about 2 hours. From time to time while baking, stir barley with a fork.

Add chopped and drained pimento with parsley to the casserole before serving.

Yield: 8 servings

Per Serving:
Calories: 117
Fat: 0.3 grams
Calories from Fat:
Carbohydrates: 25.3 grams
Protein: 3.8 grams
Cholesterol: 0 milligrams
Sodium: 9 milligrams
Dietary Fiber: 2.4 grams

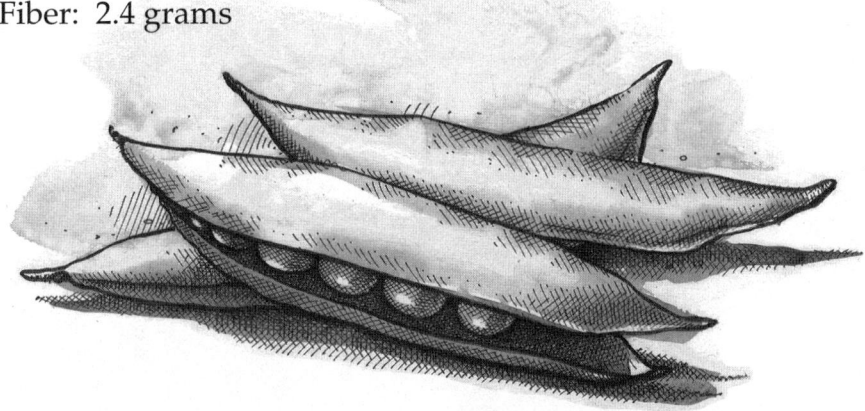

Barley-Vegetable Pilaf

2 cans fat-free, low-sodium chicken broth
1 cup pearled barley
1 cup chopped onions
1/2 cup sliced green onions
1/2 cup grated carrot
1/4 teaspoon garlic powder
1/4 teaspoon sea salt
1 tablespoon fresh parsley, chopped

Bring broth to a boil in medium saucepan. Add barley. Cover, reduce heat, and simmer 15 minutes.

Stir in next 5 ingredients. Cover and continue cooking 10 minutes or until barley is tender and broth is absorbed. Stir in parsley and serve.

Yield: 4 cups

Per Serving:
Calories: 214
Fat: 1 gram
Carbohydrate: 47 grams
Protein: 6 grams
Cholesterol: 0 milligrams
Sodium: 100 milligrams
Dietary Fiber: 10 grams

Basil Brown Rice

2 cups brown rice
4 cups water
1/2 cup chopped onions
3 tablespoons fresh basil
1/2 teaspoon sea salt

Combine all ingredients in a baking dish. Cover and bake in a 350 degree oven for 50 to 60 minutes.

Per Serving:
Calories: 259
Fat: 2 grams
Carbohydrate: 54 grams
Protein: 6 grams
Cholesterol: 0 milligrams
Sodium: 206 milligrams
Dietary Fiber: 4 grams

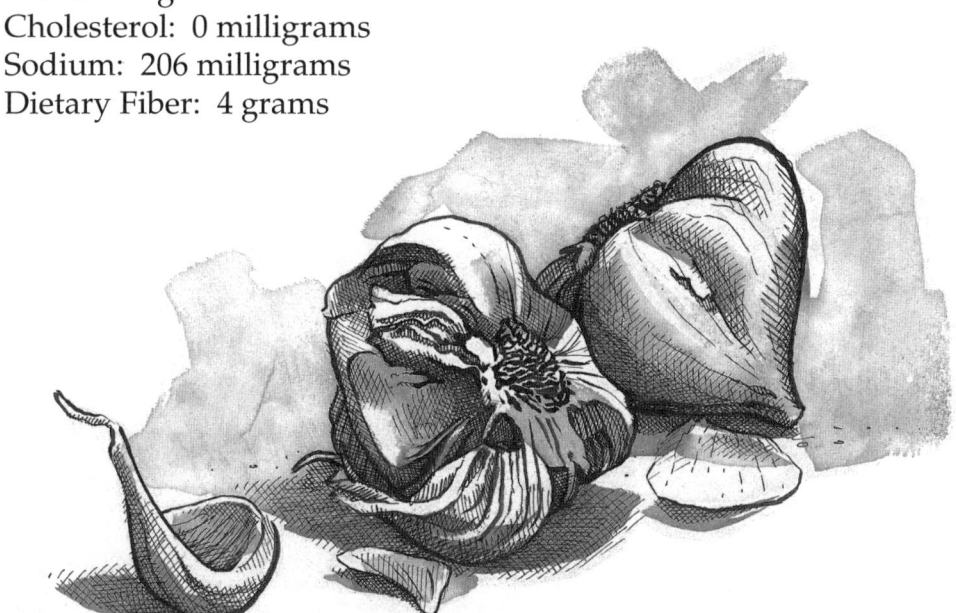

Brown Rice Pilaf

1 tablespoon olive oil
2 tablespoons onions, finely chopped
1 clove garlic, minced
1 cup brown rice
2 1/4 cups fat-free chicken broth

3 sprigs fresh parsley
1 sprig fresh thyme or 1/4 teaspoon dried
1 bay leaf
Salt and pepper to taste

Saute onions and garlic in saucepan in olive oil until wilted. Add rice and stir briefly over low heat until the grains are coated.

Stir in chicken broth and herbs, making sure there are no lumps in the rice. Bring to a boil, cover, reduce heat, and simmer until all liquid is absorbed, about 45 minutes.

Remove parsley, thyme and bay leaf before serving. Season to taste and serve.

Yield: 4 servings

Per Serving:
Calories: 216
Fat: 5 grams
Carbohydrate: 38 grams
Protein: 5 grams
Cholesterol: 0 milligrams
Sodium: 524 milligrams
Dietary Fiber: 2 grams

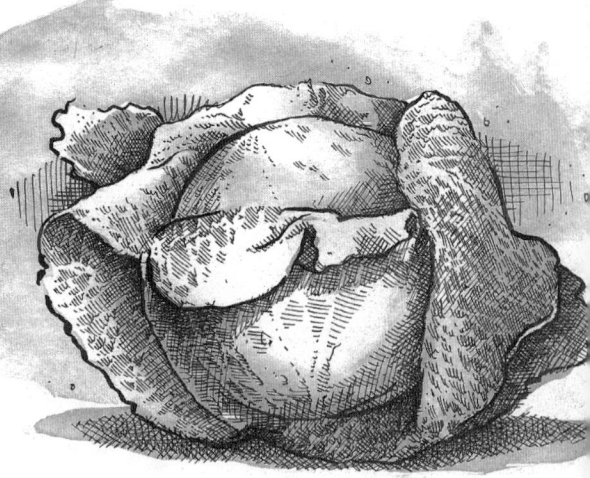

Carrot-Rice Casserole

6 large carrots, diagonally sliced
2 cups brown rice, cooked
1/3 cup finely chopped pecans
1 teaspoon olive oil
1 medium onion, chopped
1 10 oz. package "lite" soft tofu
3/4 cup nonfat milk
1/2 cup egg beaters
1/3 cup Parmesan cheese
Sea salt and pepper to taste
Vegetable cooking spray

Steam carrots until barely tender; drain. Set aside.
Combine cooked rice and pecans. Set aside.
Saute onion in olive oil until tender. Set aside.
Spray large casserole dish with vegetable cooking spray. Layer rice mixture, onions, and then carrots.
Combine tofu, milk, egg beaters, and cheese in a blender. Blend until smooth. Pour tofu mixture over layered casserole.
Bake at 350 degrees for 30 minutes or until hot and bubbly. (This is a great leftover dish which can be easily reheated.)
Yield: 8 servings

Per Serving:
Calories: 217
Fat: 9 grams
Carbohydrate: 20 grams
Protein: 15 grams
Cholesterol: 17 milligrams
Sodium: 455 milligrams
Dietary Fiber: 2 grams

Colorful Stuffed Peppers

2 medium-sized green peppers
2 medium-sized red peppers
1/2 cup chopped onion
1/4 cup chopped celery
4 large mushrooms
2 tablespoons dry white wine
3/4 cup cooked brown rice

1 (8-ounce) can whole kernel corn, drained
1/2 cup reduced-fat Sharp Cheddar cheese
1 teaspoon garlic powder
1/2 teaspoon rosemary
1 teaspoon parsley flakes

Cut off the tops of peppers and remove seeds. Chop pepper tops; reserve 1/3 cup chopped pepper.

Combine 1/3 cup pepper and next 4 ingredients in medium skillet. Saute vegetables over medium heat until tender.

Remove from heat and add next 6 ingredients; mix well.

Stuff peppers with mixture and place in shallow baking dish.

Bake at 350 degrees for 30 minutes.

Yield: 4 servings (For color, you may want to serve 1/2 green pepper and 1/2 red pepper as a serving)

Per Serving:
Calories: 192
Fat: 6 grams
Carbohydrate: 25 grams
Protein: 11 grams
Cholesterol: 20 milligrams
Sodium: 284 milligrams
Dietary Fiber: 3 grams

Italian Baked Rice

3 cups cooked brown rice
1/4 cup chopped pimento
1/4 cup chopped green pepper
1/3 cup chopped onion
1/4 teaspoon paprika
1 teaspoon soy sauce
1 1/2 cups cooked or canned tomatoes
1/4 cup Parmesan cheese

Combine first 6 ingredients. Turn into 1 1/2-quart baking dish that has been sprayed with cooking spray.
Spread tomatoes on rice.
Sprinkle Parmesan cheese on top.
Bake at 350 degrees for 30 minutes.
Yield: 4-6 servings

Per Serving:
Calories: 143
Fat: 2 grams
Carbohydrate: 27 grams
Protein: 5 grams
Cholesterol: 3 milligrams
Sodium: 197 milligrams
Dietary Fiber: 3 grams

Lemon-Dill Rice

1 cup brown rice
2 cups water
2 tablespoons dill weed
2 tablespoons minced lemon zest
Vegetable cooking spray

Combine all ingredients in a baking dish sprayed with vegetable cooking spray. Cover and bake in a 350 degree oven for 50 to 60 minutes, or until rice has absorbed all the liquid.
Yield: 4 servings

Per Serving:
Calories: 194
Fat: 1 gram
Carbohydrate: 41 grams
Protein: 5 grams
Cholesterol: 0 milligrams
Sodium: 22 milligrams
Dietary Fiber: 3 grams

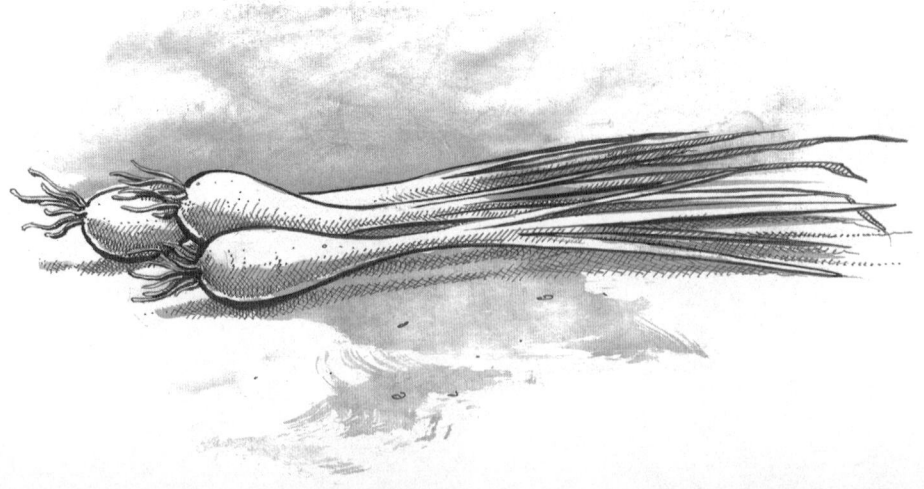

Mandarin Orange Millet

1/2 cup whole millet, rinsed well and drained
2 2/3 cup water
1/4 teaspoon sea salt
1/4 cup brown rice syrup
1 small can mandarin oranges

Combine first 3 ingredients in small saucepan and bring to a boil.
Simmer until all liquid is absorbed, about 30-35 minutes.
Remove from heat and add brown rice syrup and mandarin oranges.
Serve immediately.
Yield: 4 servings

Per Serving:
Calories: 156
Fat: 1 gram
Carbohydrate: 64 grams
Protein: 3 grams
Cholesterol: 0 milligrams
Sodium: 164 milligrams
Dietary Fiber: 3 grams

Mexican Rice

1 large can Del Monte Original stewed tomatoes, unsalted
1/2 cup long grain brown rice, uncooked
1/2 cup water
1/2-1 teaspoon chili powder

Combine all ingredients in a medium saucepan and bring to a boil. Cover and reduce heat.
Simmer 30-40 minutes or until rice is tender and liquid is absorbed.
Yield: 3 servings

Per Serving:
Calories: 141
Fat: 1 gram
Carbohydrate: 29 grams
Protein: 3 grams
Cholesterol: 0 milligrams
Sodium: 15 milligrams
Dietary Fiber: 2 grams

Millet Stuffed Squash

2 large yellow squash
1 medium onion, chopped
2 cloves garlic, chopped
1 tablespoon olive oil
1/2 cup millet, rinsed and drained
2 2/3 cup water
1 tablespoon fresh basil, chopped
1/4 - 1/2 teaspoon oregano
1/4 cup egg beaters
Fresh Parmesan Cheese (optional)

Parboil whole squash in water to cover until slightly tender. Remove from water and cool slightly. Scoop out pulp to within 1/4-inch from the sides so that the shells can be stuffed. Set aside shells and pulp.

Saute onion and garlic in olive oil until tender. Set aside.

Cook millet in water with basil and oregano until all liquid is absorbed, about 30-35 minutes.

Combine reserved pulp, sauteed vegetables, millet, and egg beaters in large bowl, mixing well.

Mound mixture into squash shells and place in 1/2-inch of water in a shallow baking dish. If desired, sprinkle lightly with Parmesan cheese.

Bake at 350 degrees for 30 minutes.

Yield: 4 servings

Per Serving:
Calories: 71
Fat: 4 grams
Carbohydrate: 6 grams
Protein: 3 grams
Cholesterol: 0 milligrams
Sodium: 44 milligrams
Dietary Fiber: 0 grams

Millet Supreme

1 tablespoon olive oil
1 medium onion, chopped
1/2- 1 cup chopped celery
2 cloves garlic, minced

1/4 teaspoon rosemary
1/4 teaspoon oregano
1/4 teaspoon thyme
1 1/2 cups cooked millet

Heat oil in large skillet and saute onion, celery, and garlic until tender.
Add seasonings to vegetables and cook for another minute.
Add millet and stir well. Serve.
Yield: 4 servings

Variations: #1: Try adding 1 tomato, cored and chopped, and 2 carrots, sliced fine, to the vegetables that you saute.
#2: Try substituting rice or quinoa for the millet.

Per Serving:
Calories: 133
Fat: 2 grams
Carbohydrate: 25 grams
Protein: 4 grams
Cholesterol: 0 milligrams
Sodium: 29 milligrams
Dietary Fiber: 2 grams

Orange-Herb Rice

2 tablespoons nonfat chicken broth
2 tablespoons onion, chopped
2 cups water
1/2 teaspoon orange rind, grated
1/2 cup fresh orange juice

1/2 teaspoon sea salt
1/8 teaspoon marjoram
1/8 teaspoon thyme
1 cup long-grain brown rice, uncooked

Saute onion in chicken broth until tender.

Add next 6 ingredients and bring to a boil.

Add rice, stirring well, and return to a boil. Reduce heat, cover, and simmer 30-40 minutes or until rice is done and all liquid is absorbed.

Fluff with a fork and serve.

Yield: 4 servings

Per Serving:
Calories: 207
Fat: 2 grams
Carbohydrate: 43 grams
Protein: 5 grams
Cholesterol: 0 milligrams
Sodium: 308 milligrams
Dietary Fiber: 3 grams

Quinoa and Squash Casserole

1 cup quinoa
2 cups fresh orange juice
1/2 cup onion, finely chopped
1 cup butternut squash, chopped very small
1/2 teaspoon sea salt
1 tablespoon fresh parsley

   Wash quinoa thoroughly.
   Combine all ingredients in a 2-quart baking dish.
   Cover and bake in 350 degree oven for 30 minutes or until quinoa has absorbed all the liquid.
   Yield: 6 servings

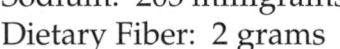

Per Serving:
Calories: 135
Fat: 2 grams
Carbohydrate: 27 grams
Protein: 4 grams
Cholesterol: 0 milligrams
Sodium: 203 milligrams
Dietary Fiber: 2 grams

Spinach and Rice Casserole

1 medium onion, chopped
1 medium red pepper, chopped
2 cloves garlic, chopped
1/3 cup plus 2 tablespoons fat-free chicken broth
2 egg whites
1 tablespoon fresh basil, chopped
2 cups fresh spinach, steamed and drained
1 cup cooked brown rice
Vegetable cooking spray

Saute first 3 ingredients in 2 tablespoons chicken broth. Set aside.

Combine 1/3 cup chicken broth, egg whites, and basil in a large mixing bowl and stir well.

Add spinach, rice and sauteed vegetables. Mix well.

Spoon into a glass baking dish that has been coated with vegetable cooking spray.

Bake at 350 degrees for 30-35 minutes.

Yield: 4 servings

Per Serving:
Calories: 104
Fat: 1 gram
Carbohydrate: 19 grams
Protein: 7 grams
Cholesterol: 0 milligrams
Sodium: 186 milligrams
Dietary Fiber: 4 grams

Sweet Brown and Wild Rice With Sugar Snaps and Sweet Peppers

1 cup brown rice, uncooked
1/4 cup wild rice, uncooked
3 cups fat-free chicken broth
1 clove garlic, minced
1 green onion, chopped
1 cup fresh sugar snap pea pods
1 medium red pepper, cut into short, thin strips
1 tablespoon honey

Combine rice and chicken broth in medium saucepan and bring to a boil.
Cover, reduce heat, and simmer for 40 minutes.
Add pea pods, pepper strips, and honey to rice and cover. Finish cooking rice until all liquid is absorbed.
Fluff rice and serve.
Yield: 6 servings

Per Serving:
Calories: 164
Fat: 1 gram
Carbohydrate: 35 grams
Protein: 4 grams
Cholesterol: 0 milligrams
Sodium: 4 milligrams
Dietary Fiber: 2 grams

Tomato-Millet Casserole

3 cups cooked millet
1 medium onion, finely chopped
1 clove garlic, minced

1 (16 ounce) NO SALT ADDED, can stewed tomatoes with liquid
1 tablespoon fresh basil, chopped
1 tablespoon fresh parsley, chopped

Combine all ingredients in a 1 1/2 quart baking dish.
Bake for 1 hour in a 350 degree oven.
Serve immediately.
Yield: 4 servings

Per Serving:
Calories: 263
Fat: 2 grams
Carbohydrate: 54 grams
Protein: 8 grams
Cholesterol: 0 milligrams
Sodium: 256 milligrams
Dietary Fiber: 3 grams

CHAPTER NINE

Vegetarian Main Dishes

(Beans, Grains, Pasta, & Pizza)

"Also take for yourself wheat, barley, beans, lentils, millet, and spelt; put them in a vessel, and make bread of them for yourself."

(Ezekiel 4:9)

VEGETARIAN MAIN DISHES

BEANS AND LENTILS

Beans, peas and lentils are the fruit of leguminous plants found within pods. Legumes, such as lentils are also called "pulses" and are quite delicious. Esau sold his bithright to Jacob for a bowl of lentil stew (Genesis 25:29-34) and the prophet, Daniel, ate pulses (lentils) while in captivity (Daniel 1:12). Beans and lentils were cultivated in the Tigris-Euphrates Valley nearly four thousand years ago. They are considered "poor man's meat." There is nothing poor about their high **nutritional level of** protein **and their** low cost **will keep many a person "out of the poorhouse." Beans and lentils high in fiber (about 9 grams per 1/2 cup) and very low in fat.**

Beans and lentils store easily, as do grains and will help any family reduce their total food bill! Store in a cool, dark place in tightly closed canisters or jars.

INSERT: Chart from page 25 of: BREAKING THE FAT BARRIER entitled "Cooking time for beans and legumes"

Barley-Bulgur Vegetable Casserole

2 medium carrots, halved lengthwise and sliced thinly
1 cup canned black beans, rinsed and drained
1 cup frozen whole kernel corn
1 cup fat-free chicken broth
1/2 cup pearled barley
1/3 cup snipped parsley
1/4 cup bulgur
1/4 cup chopped onion
1/4 teaspoon garlic salt
1/2 cup reduced-fat cheddar cheese (optional)

Combine all ingredients, except cheese, in a 1 1/2-quart casserole.

Cover and bake in a 350 degree oven about 1 hour until barley and bulgur are tender. Stir halfway through the baking time.

Remove from oven and sprinkle with cheese.

Cover and let stand until cheese melts.

Yield: 6 side dish servings or 4 main dish servings

Per Serving:
Calories: 208
Fat: 4 grams
Carbohydrate: 33 grams
Protein: 12 grams
Cholesterol: 14 milligrams
Sodium: 352 milligrams
Dietary Fiber: 7 grams

Barley Vegetable Chili

1 tablespoon olive oil
1 medium onion, chopped
2 cloves garlic, minced
1/4 cup green pepper, chopped
1/2 teaspoon chili powder
1/8 teaspoon ground cumin
1 (28-ounce) can plum tomatoes
1 yellow squash, sliced into 1/2-inch thick slices
1 (16-ounce) can red kidney beans, drained and rinsed
1/3 cup pearled barley, cooked

Heat oil in large, nonstick saucepan. Add onion and garlic and saute 5 minutes.
Stir in next 5 ingredients, breaking up tomatoes with spoon.
Cover and simmer over medium-low heat for 15 minutes.
Add kidney beans and barley. Cover and cook for 5 minutes.
Serve with a dollop of plain nonfat yogurt and fresh chopped chives.
Yield: 4 servings

Note: This chili is a great topping for a baked potato and it also freezes well!

Per Serving:
Calories: 165
Fat: 1 gram
Carbohydrate: 31 grams
Protein: 9 grams
Cholesterol: 0 milligams
Sodium: 344 milligrams
Dietary Fiber: 2 grams

Black Bean Burritos

2 fat-free flour tortillas
1/2 cup Garlic Bean Dip (see recipe)*
2 tablespoons minced onion
1/4 cup shredded reduced-fat Monterey Jack cheese
1 tomato, diced
Shredded lettuce
Nonfat salsa

Spread half of bean dip down the center of each tortilla.
Sprinkle with onions and cheese. Roll to enclose filling.
Place seam side down in baking dish and bake at 350 degrees for 8-10 minutes, or until warmed through.
Unroll and top filling with diced tomato, shredded lettuce, and salsa.
Yield: 2 servings

*Variation: In place of the bean dip you may use canned black beans that have been rinsed and drained or instant black beans that you just add boiling water to. (Sometimes when I am in a hurry, I warm my tortillas in the microwave and then add the warm beans and the additional toppings, roll, and serve.)

Per Serving:
Calories: 281
Fat: 5 grams
Carbohydrate: 44 grams
Protein: 15 grams
Cholesterol: 8 milligrams
Sodium: 218 milligrams
Dietary Fiber: 10 grams

Broccoli and Sun-Dried Tomatoes With Linguine

4-5 cups broccoli florets
8 ounces linguine
1 tablespoon olive oil, divided
2 large cloves garlic, minced
1/4 cup coarsely chopped sun-dried tomatoes
1/4 cup chopped fresh basil
Grated Parmesan cheese

Cook broccoli in a large saucepan of boiling water for about 2 minutes or until tender-crisp. Drain and rinse with cold water. Drain well and chop coarsely.

Cook linguine according to package directions. Drain and transfer to a large serving bowl. Toss with 2 teaspoons olive oil.

Saute garlic in heavy skillet in 1 teaspoon olive oil for a few seconds. Add broccoli and salt and pepper to taste. Saute for about 2 minutes or until heated through.

Add broccoli and garlic to pasta in large bowl and toss.

Add sun-dried tomatoes and basil. Toss again.

Sprinkle with Parmesan cheese and serve hot or at room temperature.

Yield: 4 servings

Per Serving:
Calories: 274
Fat: 3 grams
Carbohydrate: 32 grams
Protein: 5 grams
Cholesterol: 2 milligrams
Sodium: 147 milligrams
Dietary Fiber: 0 grams

Easy Spinach Lasagna

1 (15 ounce) can kidney beans, rinsed and drained
1 (16 ounce) can tomatoes
3 cups no-salt tomato sauce
1 tablespoon chopped parsley
1 teaspoon salt
1 teaspoon honey
3 cloves garlic
1/2 teaspoon pepper
1/2 teaspoon oregano
2 (10-ounce) packages frozen spinach, thawed and drained
1 (15-ounce) container part-skim ricotta cheese
1/4 cup egg beaters
10 lasagna noodles, cooked
1 cup shredded part-skim mozzarella cheese
1/4 cup grated Parmesan cheese
Vegetable cooking spray

Combine first 9 ingredients in a blender or food processor.
Process until smooth.
Pour into large saucepan and bring to boil. Reduce heat and simmer for 30 minutes. Set aside.
Combine spinach, ricotta cheese and egg beaters; mixing well. Set aside.
Cook lasagna noodles according to package directions.
Spray a 13- x 9- x 2-inch baking dish with cooking spray.
Spread 1 cup of sauce in bottom of baking dish.
Arrange 3 noodles over sauce and spoon half of the spinach mixture over noodles. Top with sauce and half of mozzarella cheese.
Repeat noodle, spinach, sauce, and cheese layer.
End with another layer of noodle, sauce, and Parmesan cheese.
Bake at 350 degrees for 40 to 50 minutes until lightly browned and bubbling. Allow to stand for 15 minutes before serving.
Yield: 8 servings

Per Serving:
Calories: 299
Carbohydrate: 38 grams
Cholesterol: 27 milligrams
Dietary Fiber: 5 grams
Fat: 8 grams
Protein: 21 grams
Sodium: 1382 milligrams

Eggplant-Couscous Rolls

2 (1 pound) eggplants
1 cup whole wheat couscous
1/2 teaspoon dried thyme
1 teaspoon olive oil
1/2 cup crumbled feta cheese
1 1/2 cups fresh tomatoes, chopped
1 teaspoon Italian seasoning
Vegetable cooking spray

Trim both ends of the eggplants. Cut eggplants lengthwise into 1/3-inch-thick slices.

Arrange eggplant slices in a single layer on baking sheets that have been sprayed with vegetable cooking spray. Bake at 425 degrees for 10 minutes, turn eggplant slices over and bake for about 10-15 minutes longer or until lightly browned and tender.

Bring 1 1/2 cups water to a boil. Stir in couscous, thyme, and olive oil. Remove from heat, cover, and let stand for 5 minutes, or until water is absorbed. Uncover and cool for 15 minutes. With a fork, stir in feta cheese.

Lightly coat a 9x13-inch baking dish with cooking spray. Put some of the couscous mixture in the center of each eggplant slice. Roll up the eggplant slices firmly around the filling and place, seam-side down, in baking dish. Cover and bake for 15 minutes.

Heat tomatoes and Italian seasoning in small saucepan over medium heat for 10-15 minutes. Spoon over cooked eggplant rolls and serve.

Yield: 4 servings

Per Serving:
Calories: 344
Fat: 8 grams
Carbohydrate: 57 grams
Protein: 13 grams
Cholesterol: 25 milligrams
Sodium: 541 milligrams
Dietary Fiber: 8 grams

Family Favorite Low-Fat Pizza

Crust:
- 1 package active dry yeast, (preferably rapid-rise type)
- 3/4 cup warm water, (110-115 degrees)
- 1 tablespoon honey
- 1 cup whole wheat or spelt flour
- 1 1/2 cups all-purpose flour

Toppings:
- 1/2 bunch fresh spinach, washed, dried and chopped
- 1 medium onion, sliced
- 1 clove garlic, minced
- 1 cup (4-ounces) part-skim mozzarella cheese, grated
- Vegetable cooking spray

Combine warm water, honey, and yeast in mixing bowl; stir well. Cover and let set for 5 minutes.

Add half of flours; stir, then beat with an electric mixer for 3 minutes at medium speed.

Gradually stir in remaining flour by hand to make firm dough.

Knead on floured surface for 5 minutes until dough is elastic and soft but not at all sticky. **(This is a great upper body workout!)** If you have an electric mixer with dough hooks, add flours gradually to liquid and it will knead it all for you.

Cover, let rise in warm, draft-free place until dough is doubled, about 30-45 minutes.

Spray 15-inch pizza pan with vegetable cooking spray. Turn risen dough onto pan. Pat and stretch dough to fit pan.

Spread pizza crusts with pizza sauce. (See Pizza Sauce recipe).

Saute onions and garlic in 1-2 tablespoons water until tender. Arrange on top of pizza sauce and place chopped spinach, uncooked, on top of onions and garlic. Sprinkle with grated cheese.

Bake at 450 degrees about 12-15 minutes until crust is golden brown. Slice and serve.

Yield: 8 slices

<u>Per slice:</u>
Calories: 195
Carbohydrate: 34 grams
Cholesterol: 8 milligrams
Dietary Fiber: 3 grams

Fat: 3 grams
Protein: 9 grams
Sodium: 85 milligrams

Grain Burgers

(These are a great substitute for the traditional hamburger when served in a bun with all the fixins!)

1 onion, finely chopped*
1 stalk celery, finely chopped*
2 carrots, finely chopped*
1 green pepper, finely chopped*
2 cloves garlic, chopped*
2 tablespoons fat-free
   chicken or vegetable broth
2 teaspoons Worcestershire
   sauce
1/2 teaspoon dried basil
1/2 cup oatmeal
3 cups cooked brown rice
2 egg whites, lightly beaten
2 tablespoons olive oil

Saute first 5 ingredients in broth until tender. Season with Worcestershire sauce and basil.

Blend oatmeal in blender for 1-2 minutes until it resembles flour. Add oatmeal and rice to vegetables and mix well.

Add egg whites, mix well, and form into 12 patties. (At this point, you can place patties on a cookie sheet, put in freezer, and freeze until firm. Remove, individually wrap, and freeze for later use.)

Heat 1 tablespoon oil in large nonstick skillet and cook patties til browned on both sides. Add other tablespoon of olive oil as needed.

Yield: 12 servings

*Note: When I'm in a hurry, I throw these ingredients in my blender and chop them all up together.

Per Serving:
Calories: 83
Carbohydrate: 15 grams
Cholesterol: 0 milligrams
Dietary Fiber: 2 grams
Fat: 2 grams
Protein: 2 grams
Sodium: 26 milligrams

Grain Roast

1/2 cups cooked kidney beans*
3/4 cup rolled oats, uncooked
1 cup brown rice, cooked
6 raw almonds, chopped
1/4 cup egg beaters
1 small onion, chopped

1 cup tomato sauce,
    NO SALT ADDED
1/8 tsp. basil
1/8 tsp. thyme
1/4 tsp. garlic powder
sea salt and pepper to taste
Vegtable cooking spray

Combine all ingredients, except cooking spray, in a large mixing bowl; slightly mashing beans. Mix well.

Press into a loaf pan that has been sprayed with vegetable cooking spray.

Bake 45-60 minutes at 350 degrees.

Slice and serve.

Yield: 6 servings

*__Note:__ If using canned kidney beans, try to find the ones with the lowest salt content.

Per Serving:
Calories: 140
Fat: 1.5 grams
Carbohydrate: 25 grams
Protein: 6 grams
Cholesterol: 0 milligrams
Sodium: 11 milligrams
Dietary Fiber: 5 grams

Italian Vegetable Pie

(This is a family favorite. It makes a great luncheon dish too.)

1 small cabbage	2 10-ounce packages frozen spinach, thawed and drained
2 tablespoons fat-free chicken broth	1 cup skim-milk ricotta cheese
1 teaspoon Worcestershire sauce	Fresh ground nutmeg
	2 egg whites, lightly beaten
1 small onion, finely chopped	3/4 cup salt-free Italian tomato sauce
2 small carrots, finely chopped	
3 cloves garlic, minced	2 tablespoons Parmesan cheese
1/4 cup chopped fresh basil	Vegetable cooking spray

Parboil cabbage for 20 minutes. Drain and separate cabbage leaves. Do not tear leaves.

Arrange cabbage leaves, overlapping, around the bottom and sides of a glass pie plate that has been sprayed lightly with vegetable cooking spray. (The cabbage leaves should extend at least 1-inch over the edge of the pie plate.) Set aside.

Saute in chicken broth and worcestershire sauce the next 3 ingredients until tender.

Add basil and spinach; blend well.

Cool slightly and add next 3 ingredients mixing well.

Spoon vegetable mixture into pie plate and curl cabbage leaves over the filling.

Spoon tomato sauce over the top of the pie and sprinkle with Parmesan cheese.

Bake at 325 degrees for 30 minutes.

Yield: 8 servings

Per Serving:
Calories: 135
Carbohydrate: 19 grams
Cholesterol: 11 milligrams
Dietary Fiber: 7 grams
Fat: 4 grams
Protein: 10 grams
Sodium: 321 milligrams

Laura's Lentil Stew

2 cups green lentils, uncooked
4 cups de-fatted chicken broth
4 cups water
1 large onion, diced
2 stalks celery, sliced
3 medium carrots, sliced

2 cups fresh green beans, cut in 1-inch pieces
1 cup frozen corn kernels
3 white potatoes, cubed
Sea salt and pepper to taste

Soak lentils 12-24 hours in enough water to cover. Drain and rinse lentils.

Combine soaked lentils, broth, water, onion, and celery in large Dutch oven or pot. Bring to a boil, cover, reduce heat, and simmer for 1 hour.

Add carrots and green beans and cook for another 1/2 hour.

Add corn and potatoes and cook another 1/2 hour. Season to taste.

Yield: 6 servings

Per Serving:
Calories: 180
Fat: 0 grams
Carbohydrate: 36 grams
Protein: 10 grams
Cholesterol: 0 milligrams
Sodium: 354 milligrams
Dietary Fiber: 10 grams

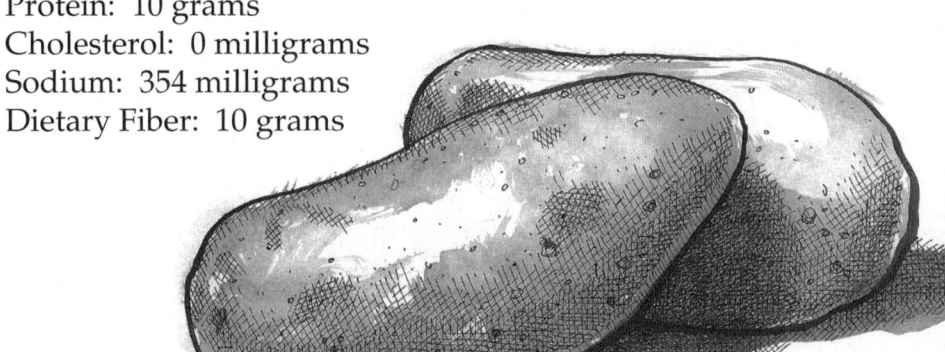

Pasta Faggioli

6 large cloves garlic, chopped
1 tablespoon olive oil
2 small ripe tomatoes, chopped

2 cans Northern Beans, rinsed and drained
8 ounces small pasta, round or curly shaped

Cook pasta in a large pan of water over high heat until tender, about 8-10 minutes. Drain well and set aside.

Saute garlic in olive oil until tender.

Add tomatoes and beans and heat thoroughly for flavors to blend, about 3 minutes.

Add pasta and toss with tomato and beans.

Yield: 4 servings

Per Serving:
Calories: 433
Fat: 6 grams
Carbohydrate: 75 grams
Protein: 24 grams
Cholesterol: 0 milligrams
Sodium: 65 milligrams
Dietary Fiber: 14 grams

Mexican Pizza

1 fat-free tortilla
1-2 tablespoons fat-free salsa
1 tablespoon chopped green chilies (optional)
1/4 cup shredded reduced-fat Monterey Jack cheese
Ground cumin (optional)
Chili powder (optional)

Bake tortilla at 400 degrees for 4-6 minutes until it begins to crisp.
Remove from oven and top with salsa, chopped chilies, and cheese.
Sprinkle <u>lightly</u> with cumin and chili powder if desired.
Yield: 1 serving

Per Serving:
Calories: 136
Fat: 5 grams
Carbohydrate: 13 grams
Protein: 9 grams
Cholesterol: 15 milligrams
Sodium: 123 milligrams
Dietary Fiber: 1 gram

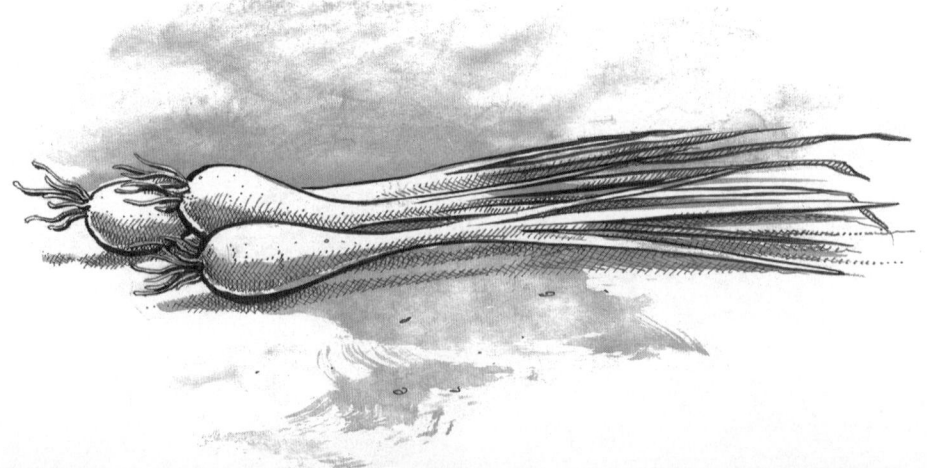

Pasta Madelena

1 medium red onion,
  finely chopped
2-3 cloves garlic, chopped
1 small green pepper,
  finely chopped
1 tablespoon olive oil
1/2 can Goya Great Northern
  beans

1/2 can Goya pink beans
5 medium fresh tomatoes,
  chopped
A <u>light</u> sprinkle of dried
  parsley, basil, and oregano
1 lb. curly pasta, (whole
  wheat or flavored)

Saute onion and garlic in large skillet in olive oil until soft.

Add green peppers and cook until tender; adding small amounts of water if needed.

Add beans that have been rinsed and drained. Cook for 5-7 minutes so beans are able to absorb the flavors of the onion, garlic, and peppers.

Add fresh chopped tomatoes and let simmer about 25 minutes. (You do not want the beans to become mushy.)

Cook pasta according to package directions. Drain and toss with tomatoes and beans. Serve.

Yield: 6 servings

Pe**r Serving:**
Calories: 351
Fat: 5 grams
Carbohydrate: 64 grams
Protein: 15 grams
Cholesterol: 0 milligrams
Sodium: 32 milligrams
Dietary Fiber: 5 grams

Pita Pizza

1 nonfat whole wheat pita pocket
1 fresh tomato, diced
1 tablespoon fresh basil, minced*
1 scallion, finely chopped*
1/4 cup shredded low-fat mozzarella cheese

Split pita pocket in half so that you have 2 full-sized rounds.

Bake pita rounds at 400 degrees for 4-6 minutes until they begin to crisp.

Remove from oven and top with diced fresh tomatoes, basil, and scallion.

Sprinkle with mozzarella cheese and bake at 400 degrees for 3 to 5 minutes or until cheese melts.

Yield: 2 servings

*__Variation:__ You can substitute or add fresh broccoli florets, fresh spinach, or minced garlic to your pizza. The possibilities are endless!

Per Serving:
Calories: 174
Fat: 5 grams
Carbohydrate: 21 grams
Protein: 11 grams
Cholesterol: 15 milligrams
Sodium: 315 milligrams
Dietary Fiber: 3 grams

Rice-Stuffed Eggplant

2 eggplants (1 pound each)
1 tablespoon olive oil
1 cup chopped onion
1/2 cup chopped green pepper
3 cloves garlic, crushed
1 medium tomato, diced
2 tablespoons fresh parsley, finely chopped
2 tablespoons fresh basil, finely chopped
1/2 teaspoon cinnamon
2 cups cooked brown rice
1 cup part-skim mozzarella cheese
Grated Parmesan cheese (optional)

Halve eggplant lengthwise and place on nonstick baking sheet, cut side down.

Bake at 400 degrees for 20 minutes or until slightly softened. Remove from oven and set aside to cool.

Saute onions, green pepper, and garlic in olive oil until tender. (Add water if more moisture is required to saute.) Set aside.

Scoop out cooked eggplant within 1/4 inch of the sides so that the shells can be stuffed.

Chop cooked eggplant and add to onion mixture. Cook in skillet for about 10 minutes.

Stir in next 5 ingredients and mix well.

Spoon into eggplant shells, dividing evenly. (If desired, sprinkle tops with a small amount of Parmesan cheese.)

Bake at 350 degrees for 30 minutes.

Yield: 4 servings

Per Serving:
Calories: 314
Fat: 10 grams
Carbohydrate: 94 grams
Protein: 19 grams
Cholesterol: 15 milligrams
Sodium: 170 milligrams
Dietary Fiber: 10 grams

Spinach-Basil Pasta

(This dish is quick to make and your family will ask for more!)

1 tablespoon olive oil
2 cloves garlic, minced
1 medium onion, halved and sliced
3 large tomatoes, peeled and diced
1/4 cup fresh basil leaves, chopped

2 pounds fresh spinach; washed, stems removed, and chopped
1/2 teaspoon sea salt
1/4 teaspoon pepper
8 ounces pasta - Angel Hair or linguine
Grated Parmesan cheese (optional)

Prepare pasta according to package directions. Drain and set aside.

Heat oil in large skillet or wok. Add garlic and onions and stir-fry for 1-2 minutes.

Stir in tomatoes, basil, salt and pepper. Cook for 2 minutes, stirring frequently.

Add fresh spinach and cook until it wilts, about 2-3 minutes. Stir to blend with tomatoes and add pasta. Toss mixture well.

Serve and sprinkle with Parmesan cheese if desired.

Yield: 6 servings

Per Serving:
Calories: 167
Fat: 2 grams
Carbohydrate: 30 grams
Protein: 9 grams
Cholesterol: 0 milligrams
Sodium: 329 milligrams
Dietary Fiber: 5 grams

Veggie Pita Pockets

4 large leaves of romaine lettuce, torn in half
2 small carrots, shredded
1 small yellow squash, coarsely grated
1/2 cup broccoli florets
Alfalfa sprouts
1/2 cup cauliflower, chopped
2 small green onions, chopped
1 tomato, chopped
2 pieces whole wheat pita bread
2 tablespoons no-fat or lowfat dressing (see Dressings)

Cut pita bread in half and open pocket. Line each half with romaine lettuce.
Combine vegetables in large bowl and toss with dressing.
Spoon vegetable mixture between lettuce pieces.
Yield: 2 servings

Per Serving:
Calories: 197
Fat: 1 gram
Carbohydrate: 37 grams
Protein: 11 grams
Cholesterol: 0 milligrams
Sodium: 404 milligrams
Dietary Fiber: 9 grams

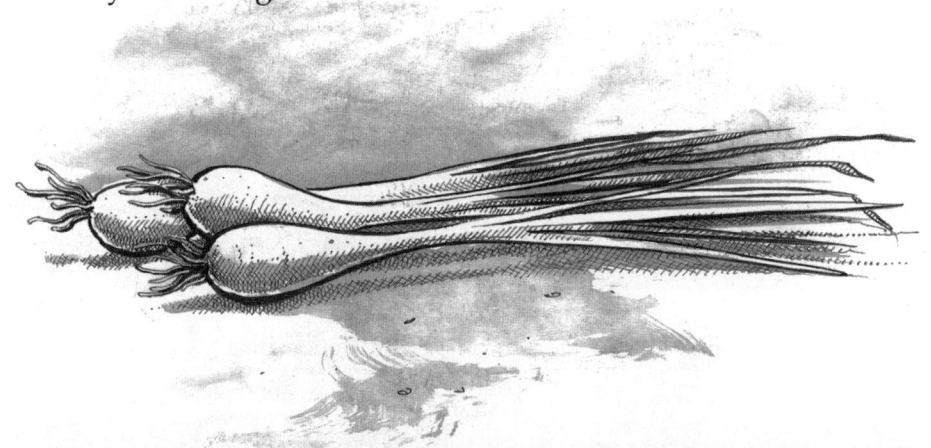

White Beans With Sage

2 cans Great Northern beans,
1 large tomato, chopped
1 medium onion, chopped
1 small green pepper
2 tablespoons grated lemon peel

1/2 teaspoon sage leaves
1 teaspoon olive oil
1/2 teaspoon salt
1/4 teaspoon pepper
1 clove garlic, minced

Rinse and drain beans. Set aside.
Combine remaining ingredients in a 2-quart saucepan. Cook over medium heat until onion is tender. Stir occasionally.
Stir in beans and cook 5 minutes, stirring occasionally, until heated through.
Yield: 6 servings

Per Serving:
Calories: 186
Fat: 1 gram
Carbohydrate: 34 grams
Protein: 11 grams
Cholesterol: 0 milligrams
Sodium: 203 milligrams
Dietary Fiber: 8 grams

CHAPTER TEN

Fish

"So they gave Him a piece of a broiled fish and some honeycomb. And He took it and ate in their presence."

(Luke 24:41-42)

COOKING FISH

The fats that all fin and scale fish (Leviticus 11:9) contain are called omega-3 fatty acids. These healthy fish that our Lord tells us we can eat, are especially rich in two fatty acids: 1) dorosahexaenoic acid (DHA) and 2) eicosapentaenoic acid (EPA). Strong scientific evidence suggests omega-3 fatty acids can decrease the incidence of coronary heart disease. These omega-3 oils are excellent sources of polyunsaturated fatty acids necessary in the production of sex hormones. Since contaminants can accumulate in fish fat, make certain the fish you eat comes from unpolluted waters. **Due to the possibility of bacterial infection, fresh fish should only be kept at room temperature for two hours.** After fresh fish are defrosted, they can only be refrigerated for two days before using. Fish should be cooked at low temperatures (300-325 degrees) in order to preserve the flavors, juices and nutrients. Fish may be broiled, baked, steamed, grilled or poached, but don't fry. Never, never, eat raw fish (Sushi bars) because of the bacterial problems associated with fish.

Dilled Salmon

4 ounce salmon steak
1 tablespoon lemon juice
1 small clove garlic, minced
1 teaspoon fresh dill, snipped
Vegetable cooking spray

Spray grill, skillet, broiler pan or baking dish with vegetable cooking spray.
Drizzle lemon juice over fish and sprinkle with garlic, and dill.
Cook about 10 minutes per inch of fish and turn after 5 minutes (except when baked)
Yield: 1 serving

Per Serving:
Calories: 177
Fat: 5 grams
Carbohydrate: 2 grams
Protein: 29 grams
Cholesterol: 76 milligrams
Sodium: 98 milligrams
Dietary Fiber: 0 grams

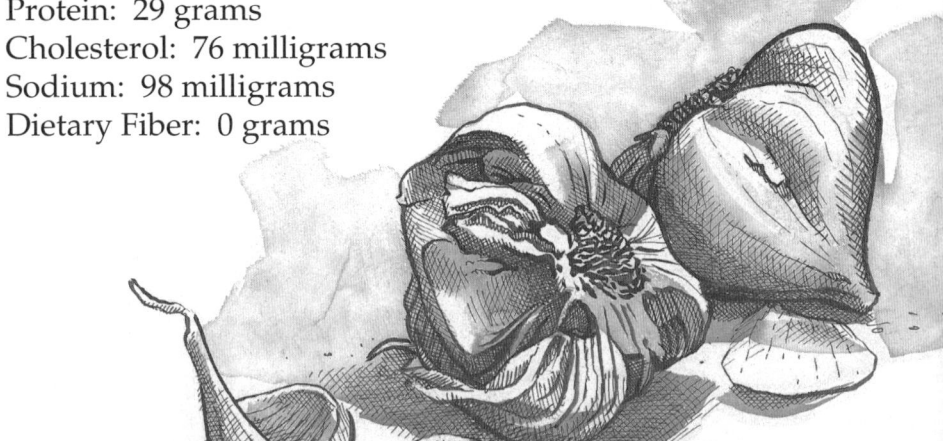

Grilled Garlic-Basil Grouper

3 lbs. grouper fillets
1/2 cup olive oil
1/3 cup tomato sauce
1/8 cup vinegar

4 cloves garlic, crushed
1/4 cup chopped fresh basil
1 teaspoon salt
1 teaspoon red pepper

Arrange fish in a large shallow dish.
Combine olive oil and next 6 ingredients. Mix well and pour over fish.
Cover and chill for 1 hour.
Remove fish from marinade and arrange on a pre-heated grill over medium heat.
Cook, covered with grill lid, for approximately 9 minutes on each side.
Yield: 6 servings

Per Serving:
Calories: 239
Fat: 5 grams
Carbohydrate: 3 grams
Protein: 44 grams
Cholesterol: 84 milligrams
Sodium: 511 milligrams
Dietary Fiber: 0 grams

Lemon-Dill Fish

2 pounds flounder fillets, or other fish of your choice
1 medium zucchini, thinly sliced
1 large lemon
Fresh snipped dill
Vegetable cooking spray

Place fish, skin side down, in baking dish that has been sprayed lightly with cooking spray.

Cook zucchini in a saucepan in a small amount of boiling water for 2 minutes or until tender.

Cut lemon in half. Slice 1/2 of the lemon into thin slices. Halve slices and reserve as garnish. Squeeze the juice from the remaining half over each serving of fish.

Top each fillet with some of the cooked zucchini and dill.

Bake fish, covered, in a 400 degree oven for 12-15 minutes or until fish flakes easily with a fork.

Serve and garnish with reserved lemon slices.

Yield: 4 servings

Per Serving:
Calories: 213
Fat: 3 grams
Carbohydrate: 2 grams
Protein: 43 grams
Cholesterol: 109 milligrams
Sodium: 185 milligrams
Dietary Fiber: 0 grams

Orange Orange Roughy

1/3 cup fresh orange juice
1 orange roughy filet
1/2 tablespoon dried tarragon
Grated rind of 1 orange
Vegetable cooking spray

Spray baking dish with vegetable cooking spray.
Pour orange juice into baking dish and place fish in juice.
Combine tarragon and orange rind in a small bowl and sprinkle over the fish, patting it lightly to form a thin crust.
Bake at 350 degrees until fish flakes when tested with a fork, 20-25 minutes.
Transfer fish to serving plate and discard cooking liquid.
Yield: 1 serving

Per Serving:
Calories: 120
Fat: 1 gram
Carbohydrate: 11 grams
Protein: 17 grams
Cholesterol: 22 milligrams
Sodium: 71 milligrams
Dietary Fiber: 0 grams

Orange Roughy Over Basil Vegetables

1 medium onion, sliced
2 small zucchini, sliced diagonally
3 tablespoons minced fresh basil
6 tablespoons fat-free chicken broth

1 1/2 pounds orange roughy fillets
1/4 teaspoon salt
1/4 teaspoon pepper
2 tomatoes, peeled and sliced
1 teaspoon olive oil

Saute first 3 ingredients in 3 tablespoons chicken broth in a large skillet over medium-high heat for 3-4 minutes or until crisp-tender.
Arrange vegetables on serving platter and keep warm.
Season fillets with salt and pepper and transfer to skillet with 1 teaspoon olive oil and 3 tablespoons chicken broth.
Arrange tomato slices on fillets and cover.
Simmer 8 to 9 minutes or until fish flakes easily with a fork.
Place fish and tomato slices over vegetables on serving platter.
Garnish with fresh basil leaves.
Yield: 6 servings

Per Serving:
Calories: 173
Fat: 9 grams
Carbohydrate: 5 grams
Protein: 18 grams
Cholesterol: 23 milligrams
Sodium: 222 milligrams
Dietary Fiber: 1 gram

Salmon Patties

4 cups cooked potatoes, that have been peeled and finely diced
1 (7 1/2-ounce) can salmon; preferably packed in water, drained, and flaked
1/3 cup finely chopped green pepper
2-3 tablespoons finely chopped onion
1 egg white, slightly beaten
Sea salt and pepper to taste
Olive oil cooking spray

Combine all ingredients except olive oil and mix well.
Shape into 12 small patties or 6 larger ones.
Cook in nonstick skillet that has been lightly sprayed with olive oil until both sides of patty are browned.
Yield: 6 servings

Per Serving:
Calories: 131
Fat: 2 grams
Carbohydrate: 18 grams
Protein: 9 grams
Cholesterol: 19 milligrams
Sodium: 89 milligrams
Dietary Fiber: 1 gram

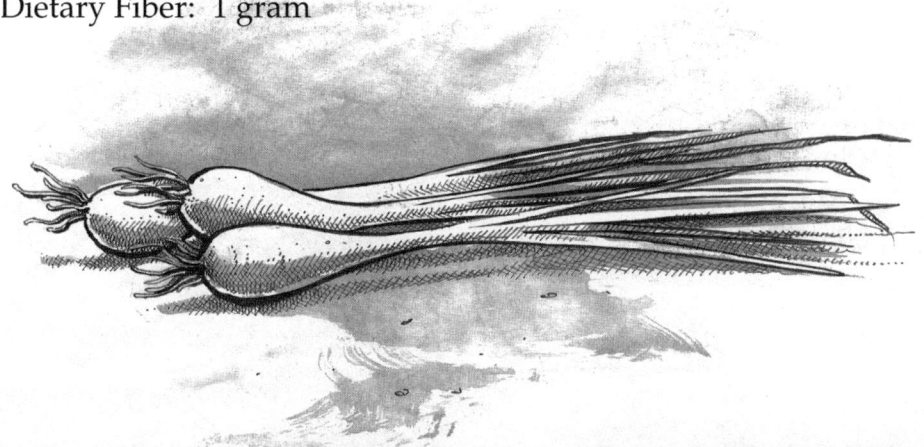

Tex-Mex Fillets

1 cup finely chopped tomatoes, seeded
1/4 cup finely chopped onion
1/4 cup finely chopped celery
1/4 cup finely chopped green pepper
2 cloves garlic, minced
2 teaspoons olive oil
1/4 cup fat-free chicken broth
1 small can of green chilies, chopped and drained
2 tablespoons lime juice
1/2 teaspoon chopped fresh cilantro
1/8 teaspoon ground cumin
1/4 teaspoon sea salt
Dash of ground red pepper
4 (4-ounce) orange roughy fillets
Vegetable cooking spray

Saute first 5 ingredients in olive oil in a medium skillet until crisp-tender.

Add next 7 ingredients; reduce heat and cook 15 minutes. Remove from heat and set aside.

Cook fillets on the grill or under the broiler for 7 to 8 minutes on each side or until fish flakes easily with a fork.

Serve fillets with vegetable mixture on top.

Yield: 4 servings

Per Serving:
Calories: 166
Fat: 6 grams
Carbohydrate: 8 grams
Protein: 18 grams
Cholesterol: 23 milligrams
Sodium: 747 milligrams
Dietary Fiber: 2 grams

Super Grouper with Orange Sauce

2 oranges, peeled and sliced into thin rounds
6 grouper fillets (about 2 lbs.)
1 tablespoon olive oil
2 tablespoons sherry (optional)
1 cup finely chopped shallots
2 garlic cloves, minced
3 tablespoons all-purpose flour
1 cup chicken broth
1 cup orange juice
1 tablespoon grated orange peel
1 1/2 teaspoons dried oregano
Salt and pepper to taste
2 tablespoons chopped parsley

Place grouper, skin-side down, on nonstick jelly-roll pan. Place pan 4 inches from broiler and broil 5-8 minutes, or until fish is cooked through. Remove from broiler and set aside.

Saute shallots and garlic in a large skillet in olive oil 3-4 minutes, or until shallots begin to brown, stirring often. Stir in flour and cook about 30 seconds.

Stir in next 6 ingredients and bring to a boil. Reduce heat slightly and cook 1-2 minutes or until slightly thickened. Stir constantly.

Add orange slices and grouper fillets, <u>skin-side up</u>. Cook 1-2 minutes or until fish is heated through and orange slices are slightly soft.

Serve fillets with orange slices and chopped parsley arranged on top.

Yield: 6 servings

<u>**Per Serving:**</u>
Calories: 240
Fat: 4 grams
Carbohydrate: 19 grams
Protein: 32 grams
Cholesterol: 56 milligrams
Sodium: 268 milligrams
Dietary Fiber: 2 grams

CHAPTER ELEVEN

Poultry

"The people asked, and He brought quail,
And satisfied them with the bread of heaven."
(Psalm 105:40)

POULTRY

COOKING TURKEY AND CHICKEN

Although chicken and turkey are lower in total fat than most red meats, there are other problems. The commercial poultry producers add synthetic hormones and antibiotics to the feed. Most commercial chickens and turkeys are cooped up for their entire lives in crowded cages and never see the light of day. Therefore, you must find "free-range" varieties that are permitted to live a more natural existence and are fed hormone-free organic grains. When boiling, baking, broiling or grilling pieces of chicken or turkey, remove the skin before cooking. If you are baking or roasting an entire bird remove the skin after cooking. Removing the skin from the white meat of chicken or turkey reduces the fat by one-half (1/2). Removing the skin from the dark meat cuts the fat by one-third (1/3). Poultry does not contain the healthful omega-3 oils of fin and scale fish.

A WARNING ABOUT ANIMAL PROTEINS

The modern plagues of heart disease and cancer are a result of excess animal protein in our diets and therefore a reduction in the frequency of these foods is recommended. Americans are eating more poultry/fish and less red meat than ever, but limiting poultry and fish to three or four times a week will go a long way towards reducing your risks of these degenerative diseases. Americans are eating two or three times the amount of protein and fat as they actually need and most of that excess comes from animal fats.

The high-energy, high-fiber, low fat complex carbohydrates (grains, beans, lentils, fruits and vegetables) are the foundation of the Genesis diet (Genesis 1:29) , not the high protein foods like poultry and fish. **By increasing the amount of grains and beans in your daily eating program, good quality protein will not be sacrificed.** The recipes contained in this cookbook will help you attain this goal.

Basil Barley Chicken

5 cups water
2/3 cup pearl barley
1/2 pound boneless chicken breasts
3/4 cup chopped carrots
3/4 cup chopped celery
1 cup chopped leeks

2-3 cloves garlic, minced
1/2 cup chopped fresh basil
1/2 cup fat-free chicken broth
6 tablespoons grated Parmesan cheese

Bring water and barley to a boil in a medium saucepan. Reduce heat, cover, and simmer until barley is tender, stirring occasionally, about 45 minutes. Drain. Transfer to a large bowl and set aside.

Broil skinless chicken breasts until cooked through, about 3 minutes on each side. Transfer chicken to a plate and cool. Shred chicken into pieces.

Combine carrots, celery, leeks, and garlic in large nonstick skillet. Cover and cook over low heat until tender, stirring frequently, about 15-20 minutes. (Add small amounts of water if vegetables begin to stick.)

Add barley, chicken, basil, broth, and 3 tablespoons Parmesan cheese. Stir until heated through. Divide among plates, sprinkle with remaining cheese, and serve.

Yield: 6 servings

Per Serving:
Calories: 169
Fat: 3 grams
Carbohydrate: 27 grams
Protein: 10 grams
Cholesterol: 20 milligrams
Sodium: 196 milligrams
Dietary Fiber: 4 grams

Chicken and Barley Casserole

3 large boneless, skinless chicken breast halves
1 tablespoon olive oil
2 tablespoons fat-free chicken broth
1 cup onion, finely chopped
2 large cloves garlic, chopped
1 green pepper, minced
1 red pepper, minced
1/2 cup minced celery
1/2 cup dry white wine
1 (28-ounce) can tomatoes, drained and chopped
1 cup barley, rinsed
3 cups fat-free chicken broth
Sea salt and pepper to taste
3 scallions, as garnish
Fresh dill sprigs as garnish

Brown chicken breasts (both sides) in large skillet using olive oil, about 3-4 minutes Season with salt and pepper if desired. Set aside.

Saute onion, garlic, peppers, and celery in 2 tablespoons chicken broth for about 5 minutes.

Add wine to the vegetables and bring to a boil. Simmer until almost all of the liquid has evaporated.

Add tomatoes, barley, and broth and return to a boil. Cover, reduce heat, and cook mixture for 25 minutes. Transfer to a casserole dish and push chicken into barley mixture.

Cover and bake at 350 degrees for 40-45 minutes. (If casserole seems to be drying out, add a small amount of chicken broth.)

Garnish with scallions and dill sprigs.

Yield: 6 servings

Per Serving:
Calories: 267
Fat: 5 grams
Carbohydrate: 33 grams
Protein: 20 grams
Cholesterol: 44 milligrams
Sodium: 670 milligrams
Dietary Fiber: 5 grams

Chicken and Pepper Stir-Fry with Almonds
(This is a hit with our children!)

2 tablespoons fat-free chicken broth
1 large green pepper, cut into 1/4-inch strips
4 boneless, skinless chicken breast halves, cut into 1/2-inch strips

2 tablespoons low-sodium soy sauce
1 tablespoon cornstarch
1/2 cup cold fat-free chicken broth
2 tablespoons white wine
12 almonds, coarsely chopped

Stir-fry green pepper in wok or heavy skillet in 2 tablespoons chicken broth for 2 minutes. Remove and set aside.

Stir-fry chicken strips 3-4 minutes. Return green pepper to the chicken in skillet.

Combine soy sauce, cornstarch, chicken broth, and wine.

Pour sauce over chicken and peppers and heat and stir gently until the sauce is thickened. Add almonds and serve at once over rice.

Yield: 6 servings

Per Serving:
Calories: 70
Fat: 3 grams
Carbohydrate: 3 grams
Protein: 6 grams
Cholesterol: 24 milligrams
Sodium: 307 milligrams
Dietary Fiber: 0 grams

Chicken Chili

3-4 cloves garlic, minced
2 cups finely chopped onion
1 tablespoon olive oil
1 1/2 lbs. boneless, skinless chicken breast halves
2 (16-ounce) cans fat-free chicken broth
3 (16-ounce) cans Great Northern beans
1 small can mild green chilies, chopped
1/2-1 teaspoon cumin*
1/2-1 teaspoon oregano*
1/8 teaspoon cayenne pepper*

Saute garlic and onion in large saucepan in olive oil until tender.

Cook chicken in water until done, about 20 minutes, then cut into bite-sized pieces.

Add chicken and remaining ingredients to garlic and onions. Simmer for 20 minutes. (Best if this is made a day ahead so flavors can blend.)

Yield: 8 servings

*__Note:__ You can adjust the seasonings to your taste - more or less.

Per Serving:
Calories: 397
Fat: 10 grams
Carbohydrate: 46 grams
Protein: 32 grams
Cholesterol: 69 milligrams
Sodium: 278 milligrams
Dietary Fiber: 10 grams

Chicken in Foil

2 (4 ounce) skinned chicken breast halves
1/4 cup sliced onion
1/2 tomato, sliced
1 medium-size baking potato, sliced

1 small carrot, sliced
1 stalk celery, sliced
1/4 teaspoon pepper
1/8 teaspoon dried tarragon
1 teaspoon lemon juice

Cut two 15x12 pieces of heavy duty foil. Place a chicken breast in center of each. Top with onion and remaining ingredients. Wrap well.
   Place on baking sheet and bake at 350 degrees for 1 hour.
   Yield: 2 servings

*I use one great big sheet of foil and 5-6 chicken breast halves and cover them with more of the vegetables and herb. Bake as above. It's great!

Per Serving:
Calories: 261
Fat: 3 grams
Carbohydrate: 28 grams
Protein: 30 grams
Cholesterol: 72 milligrams
Sodium: 100 milligrams
Dietary Fiber: 4 grams

Chicken Fajita Pita Pockets

1 clove garlic, minced
1 medium onion, chopped
1/4 cup fresh lime juice
2 teaspoons olive oil
1/4 teaspoon ground cumin
1/4 teaspoon sea salt
1 tablespoon chopped fresh cilantro
2 boneless, skinless chicken breast halves, cut into 1-inch wide strips
1 red pepper, cut in thin strips
2 whole wheat pita-pockets

Combine first 7 ingredients in medium-sized bowl. Add chicken and peppers. Cover and marinate in the refrigerator for at least 30 minutes.

Heat large nonstick skillet over medium-high heat. Saute chicken and vegetables in the marinade for 15 minutes or until chicken is done.

Place chicken mixture in pita pockets, dividing equally.

Add chopped lettuce, salsa, and nonfat plain yogurt to pita bread. Serve with black beans if desired.

Yield: 2 servings

Per Serving:
Calories: 263
Fat: 4 grams
Carbohydrate: 32 grams
Protein: 24 grams
Cholesterol: 44 milligrams
Sodium: 642 milligrams
Dietary Fiber: 6 grams

Chicken-Rice Salad

3 boneless, skinless chicken breast halves
5 medium tomatoes, cut into thin wedges
1/2 cup chopped fresh basil

1 tablespoon olive oil
1 tablespoon fresh lemon juice
1 large garlic clove, minced
3 cups cooked brown rice
Leaf lettuce

Broil or grill chicken until cooked through, about 15 minutes. Cool and cut into 1/2-inch wide strips.

Combine next 5 ingredients in large bowl and let stand at room temperature for 20 minutes.

Add rice and chicken to bowl and stir to blend. If desired, season with sea salt and pepper to taste.

Spoon salad into center of serving platter that has been lined with lettuce.

Garnish with fresh basil leaves and serve.

Yield: 4 servings

Per Serving:
Calories: 332
Fat: 6 grams
Carbohydrate: 42 grams
Protein: 18 grams
Cholesterol: 52 milligrams
Sodium: 75 milligrams
Dietary Fiber: 4 grams

Honey-Mustard Chicken

6 boneless, skinless chicken
   breast halves
3 tablespoons honey
2 tablespoons lime juice
1-1/2 tablespoons
   coarse-grained mustard
1 teaspoon olive oil

Pound chicken to 1/2-inch thickness. Place in glass baking dish.

Combine next 3 ingredients, mixing well and pour over chicken.

Marinate at room temperature for 15 minutes, turning once.

Heat olive oil in skillet over medium heat. Add chicken and cook 5 minutes per side or until chicken is cooked through and golden brown. Remove chicken from skillet and keep warm.

Add reserved marinade to skillet and cook over high heat 2 minutes or until thickened.

Spoon over chicken and serve.

Yield: 6 servings

Per Serving:
Calories: 176
Fat: 3 grams
Carbohydrate: 9 grams
Protein: 27 grams
Cholesterol: 72 milligrams
Sodium: 103 milligrams
Dietary Fiber: 0 grams

Lemon-Basil Chicken Tenders

1 garlic clove, minced
1 strip lemon zest, chopped
1/4 cup fresh basil leaves
1 tablespoon olive oil

1 pound package chicken tenders
Sea salt and pepper to taste
2 tablespoons fresh lemon juice

Chop very finely the garlic, lemon zest, and basil leaves. Set aside.

Heat oil in large skillet until hot. Add chicken tenders, a few at a time, and adjust heat so that chicken will cook steadily. Cook until lightly browned on both sides.

Sprinkle chicken with salt and pepper, if desired. Add garlic, lemon zest, and basil leaves and cook about 1 minute, stirring constantly.

Stir in lemon juice and serve.

Yield: 4 servings

Per Serving:
Calories: 158
Fat: 4 grams
Carbohydrate: 2 grams
Protein: 27 grams
Cholesterol: 72 milligrams
Sodium: 137 milligrams
Dietary Fiber: 0

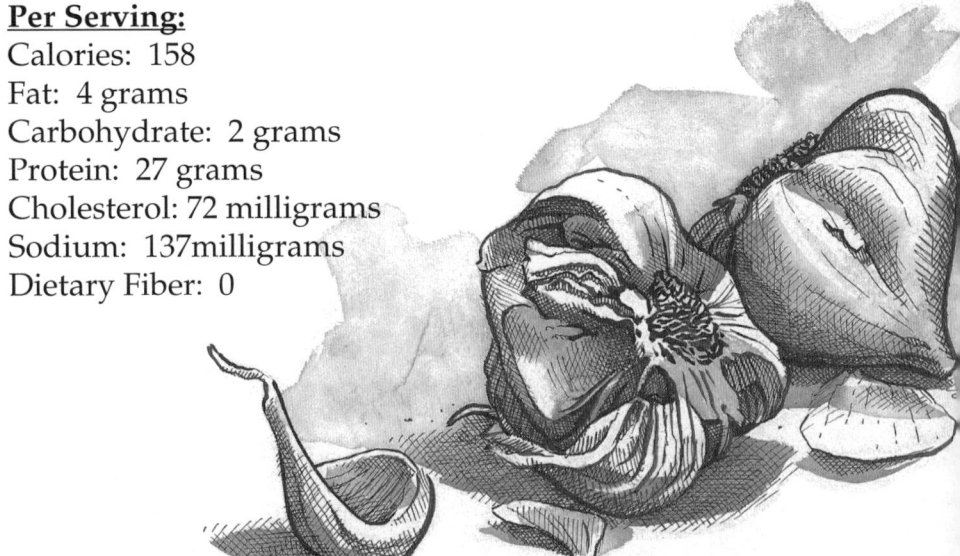

Lemon Chicken Breasts

1 tablespoon olive oil
4 chicken breast halves, skinned
1 teaspoon dried parsley flakes
1/2 teaspoon dried whole thyme
1/4 teaspoon sea salt
1 cup dry white wine
3 tablespoons lemon juice
1/4 teaspoon pepper
1/4 teaspoon paprika

Cook chicken breasts in olive oil in heavy skillet for 5 minutes on both sides. Remove chicken from skillet and place in 8-inch square baking dish.

Combine next 4 ingredients in skillet and bring to a boil. Pour over chicken.

Sprinkle chicken with lemon juice, pepper, and paprika.

Cover and bake at 400 degrees for 25 minutes or until tender.

Garnish with fresh lemon slices and fresh parsley sprigs and serve.

Yield: 4 servings

Per Serving:
Calories: 114
Fat: 4 grams
Carbohydrate: 2 grams
Protein: 9 grams
Cholesterol: 36 milligrams
Sodium: 185 milligrams
Dietary Fiber: 0 grams

Pepper Chicken and Rice

This colorful, "all-in-one-pan" dish is easy to prepare.

4 boneless, skinless chicken breast halves (1 pound)
1/2 teaspoon ground cumin
2 teaspoons olive oil
1 tablespoon low sodium soy or tamari sauce
1 medium onion, thinly sliced
1 medium green pepper, cut into thin strips
1 medium red pepper, cut into strips
2 large cloves garlic, minced
1 cup brown rice, uncooked
2 medium tomatoes, peeled, seeded, and chopped
1 1/2 cups fat-free chicken broth

Rub cumin into both sides of chicken breasts.

Heat oil and soy sauce in large skillet and add chicken breasts. Brown over medium-low heat for about 10-15 minutes until brown. Remove.

Add onion and cook over low heat until tender. Stir in peppers and garlic and cook about 5 minutes.

Add rice and saute for 2 minutes.

Stir in tomatoes and set chicken breasts on top.

Pour hot chicken broth over the top. Reduce heat to very low and cover.

Cook for 45-50 minutes or until chicken and rice are tender and the liquid is absorbed. (If all liquid is absorbed and rice is not tender yet, add a few more tablespoons of chicken broth and simmer a few more minutes.)

Yield: 4 servings

Per Serving:
Calories: 377
Carbohydrate: 49 grams
Cholesterol: 72 milligrams
Dietary Fiber: 5 grams
Fat: 5 grams
Protein: 33 grams
Sodium: 527 milligrams

Pineapple-Chicken Stir Fry

3 large boneless, skinless
    chicken breasts
1 onion, halved and sliced
1 cup celery, sliced diagonally
1 green pepper, thinly sliced
2 cups pineapple chunks,
    drained and reserve juice

Reserved pineapple juice
2 teaspoons cornstarch
1/2 teaspoon cinnamon
1 1/2 teaspoons low-sodium
    soy sauce
Olive oil cooking spray

Cut chicken breasts into 10-12 strips each.

Combine reserved pineapple juice, cornstarch, cinnamon, and soy sauce. Set aside.

Saute chicken over high heat in nonstick skillet sprayed with cooking spray. Stir constantly for 3 minutes.

Add onion, celery, and green pepper strips, cooking and stirring constantly for 2 minutes.

Add pineapple, then pineapple juice mixture. Stir and bring to a boil. Reduce and cook just until liquid is clear.

Serve over hot brown rice.

Yield: 6 servings

Per Serving:
Calories: 151
Fat: 2 grams
Carbohydrate: 17 grams
Protein: 19 grams
Cholesterol: 44 milligrams
Sodium: 107 milligrams
Dietary Fiber: 1 gram

Quinoa and Chicken

2 cups quinoa, rinsed
5 cups water
1 teaspoon salt
1/2 cup finely chopped celery
2 cloves garlic, minced
1/2 cup finely chopped onion

4 boneless, skinless chicken breasts
1/4 cup plain nonfat yogurt
1/4 cup fat-free mayonnaise
1 teaspoon chopped fresh dill and fresh chives

Combine first 6 ingredients in a large saucepan. Bring to a boil and reduce heat. Simmer over low heat for 20 minutes or until all liquid is absorbed.

Cook chicken breasts in separate pan of water, just enough to cover, for 35 to 40 minutes, until just done.

Remove chicken breasts from water and cool.

Cut chicken into small pieces and add to quinoa.

Combine yogurt, mayonnaise, dill and chives and mix well.

Add to quinoa and chicken and stir well.

Yield: 6 servings

Per Serving:
Calories: 292
Fat: 5 grams
Carbohydrate: 44 grams
Protein: 19 grams
Cholesterol: 30 milligrams
Sodium: 197 milligrams
Dietary Fiber: 4 grams

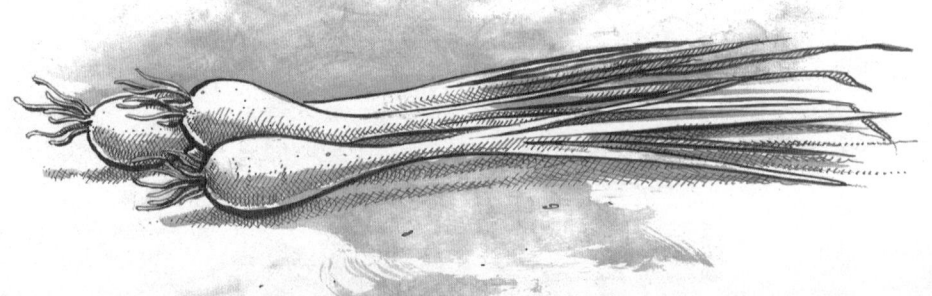

Stuffed Turkey Tenderloins

(A great dish when having guests for dinner. Serve with sauteed zucchini, yellow squash, and cherry tomatoes, for a colorful and delicious meal.)

1 1/2 pounds boneless fresh turkey breast tenderloins	2 tablespoons all-purpose flour
5 slices (3 1/2 ounces) low-fat Swiss cheese	3/4 cup skim milk
1 package frozen chopped broccoli, thawed and drained	1 tablespoon white wine
	1 tablespoon fresh chopped parsley
1 tablespoon butter	1/4 teaspoon salt
	1/8 teaspoon pepper

Slit a lengthwise pocket along the thickest side of each turkey tenderloin, cutting to within 1/2-inch of opposite side.

Cut 4 slices of cheese into strips and place in pocket of each turkey tenderloin, dividing evenly. Top with equal portions of broccoli.

Lightly spray baking dish with cooking spray. Arrange tenderloins with stuffing side towards the center of dish. Set aside.

Melt butter in medium-sized saucepan over medium-high heat. Stir in flour. Cook 1-2 minutes until smooth and bubbly, stirring often. Stir in milk and wine and cook until mixture bubbles and thickens. Stir in remaining cheese slice, parsley, salt, and pepper. Stir constantly until cheese melts.

Pour sauce evenly over turkey and cover. Bake 40 minutes; uncover and continue to bake 15-20 minutes longer, or until turkey is no longer pink in center.

Slice tenderloins crosswise and serve.

Yield: 6 servings

Per Serving:
Calories: 195
Carbohydrate: 6 grams
Cholesterol: 69 milligrams
Dietary Fiber: 1 gram
Fat: 6 grams
Protein: 29 grams
Sodium: 204 milligrams

Turkey Chili

2 pounds ground white
    turkey meat
1 medium onion, chopped
1 medium red pepper, chopped
1 - 2 stalks celery, chopped
2 cloves garlic, minced

3 cans Northern beans,
    rinsed and drained
2 large El Paso mild chunky
    salsa
1 can fat-free chicken broth

    Saute first 5 ingredients in a Dutch oven over medium-high heat until turkey meat is thoroughly cooked and vegetables are tender. Drain any grease.
    Add next 3 ingredients and simmer at least 1 hour.
    Yield: 12 servings

Per Serving:
Calories: 248
Fat: 7 grams
Carbohydrate: 24 grams
Protein: 22 grams
Cholesterol: 60 milligrams
Sodium: 238 milligrams
Dietary Fiber: 8 grams

CHAPTER TWELVE

Special Sweet Treats

"It is not good to eat much honey;
So to seek one's own glory is not glory."
(Proverbs 25:27)

SPECIAL SWEET TREATS

WHAT ARE THE BEST SWEETENERS?

Sugar, in one form or another, is the number one food additive. These "quick" sugars can contribute to tooth decay, hypoglycemia (low blood sugar), diabetes and obesity. Here is a partial list of these " sugar additives," which are essentially sugar, sugar and more sugar!

> *Barley malt syrup, beet sugar, *blackstrap molasses, brown sugar, cane sugar, caramel, corn fructose, corn sweetener, corn syrup, date sugar, dextrin, dextrose, fructose, glucose, grape sugar, high fructose corn syrup, *honey, invert sugar, lactose, maltose, manitol, *maple syrup, molasses, polydextrose, raw sugar, sorbitol, sorghum, sucanat, sucrose, and turbinado sugar.

*These sugars are somewhat better than the others in this list, but they are not the best.

YOUR BEST SWEETENERS

The ideal way to eat sugar is to eat the natural sugars contained in grains and fruits. The natural fiber in these carbohydrates allows the natural sugars to enter your blood stream SLOWLY, keeping your blood sugar relatively stable. The more you include grain dishes in your daily eating schedule, the less you will crave the "quick"sugars found in many unhealthy snacks and desserts.

When added sweeteners are called for, we recommend the grain and fruit sweeteners. The frozen fruit concentrates of apple, pineapple, orange, grape and pear are excellent sweeteners for cookies, cakes, puddings and desserts. When purchasing "store bought" cookies, look for the brands that use fruit concentrates as the sweetener. **Another fine sweetener, because it is less sweet than honey and especially good for hypoglycemics and diabetics, is brown rice syrup.** Brown rice syrup is derived from brown rice and has a very pleasant taste, without being overly sweet. Also the addition of raisins, currants or dates in hot grain cereals like oatmeal enhance the sweetness, without causing blood sugar swings. These dried fruits can be added to cookies, cakes, puddings and pies for a sweetener as well.

Almond Rice Pudding

1 cup brown rice, uncooked
1/2 cup raw almonds
3 cups water
1/4 cup maple syrup
1 teaspoon vanilla
A small piece of cinnamon stick
Pinch of sea salt

Soak rice overnight in just enough water to cover. (This softens the rice for more of a pudding texture.) Strain and set aside.

Blend almonds and 3 cups of water in blender for 1 minute. Strain through cheesecloth into a pan.

Add rice, maple syrup, cinnamon stick, vanilla, and salt. Cover and bring to a boil. Reduce heat and steep over medium low heat until all the liquid is absorbed (about 60 minutes).

Yield: 6 servings

Per Serving:
Calories: 218
Fat: 7 grams
Carbohydrate: 35 grams
Protein: 5 grams
Cholesterol: 0 milligrams
Sodium: 63 milligrams
Dietary Fiber: 2 grams

Apple Cake

5-6 peeled, cored and chopped apples
1 (6-ounce) can frozen apple juice concentrate
2/3 cup ripe bananas, mashed
1/2 cup raisins
1 1/2 cups whole wheat flour*
1 1/4 cups unbleached all-purpose flour*
1 cup Grape-Nuts (optional)
2 teaspoons Rumford aluminum-free baking powder
2 teaspoons baking soda
2 teaspoons cinnamon
1/8 teaspoon nutmeg
1/8 teaspoon allspice
4 egg whites, stiffly beaten
1 1/2 teaspoons vanilla extract

Combine apples, apple juice concentrate, bananas, and raisins in a large mixing bowl.

Combine next 7 ingredients and sift into apple mixture. Stir until flour disappears.

Fold in stiffly beaten egg whites and vanilla.

Pour into a heavy nonstick bundt pan that has been sprinkled with Grape-Nuts.

Bake at 325 degrees for 1 1/2 hours. (If top begins to brown too much, cover with foil and continue baking.)

Yield: 24 slices

Per Serving:
Calories: 114
Fat: 0 grams
Carbohydrate: 26 grams
Protein: 3 grams
Cholesterol: 0 milligrams
Sodium: 150 milligrams
Dietary Fiber: 2 grams

Apple Pie Dessert Topping

2 cups unsweetened apple juice, divided
1 1/2 peeled and finely chopped apple
1 tablespoon brown rice syrup
1/4 teaspoon apple pie spice
2 tablespoons cornstarch

Combine 1 3/4 cups apple juice and next 3 ingredients in a saucepan. Bring to boil, reduce heat, and simmer 5-8 minutes or until apples are slightly tender.

Dissolve cornstarch in remaining apple juice and stir into hot mixture.

Cook over medium heat, stirring constantly, until smooth and thickened.

Cool and serve over Frozen Vanilla Nonfat Yogurt or even over Spiced Millet (page 57).

Yield: 2 1/2 cups

Per Tablespoon Serving:
Calories: 10
Fat: 0 grams
Carbohydrate: 3 grams
Protein: 0 grams
Cholesterol: 0 milligrams
Sodium: 0 milligrams
Dietary Fiber: 0 grams

Blueberry Dessert Topping

1 1/2 cups unsweetened grape juice, divided
2 cups fresh blueberries, divided
1 tablespoon frozen unsweetened orange juice concentrate, thawed and undiluted
1/8 teaspoon ground cinnamon
1/8 teaspoon ground ginger
1 tablespoon plus 2 teaspoons cornstarch

Combine 1 cup grape juice, 1 cup blueberries, and next 3 ingredients in a saucepan. Bring to a boil, reduce heat, and simmer about 3 minutes or until blueberries pop.

Combine cornstarch and remaining grape juice; stir into fruit mixture. Bring to a boil, and cook 1 minute; stirring constantly.

Cool and stir in remaining blueberries.

Serve over Frozen Vanilla Nonfat Yogurt.

Yield: 2 1/2 cups

<u>**Per Tablespoon Serving:**</u>
Calories: 12
Fat: 0 grams
Carbohydrate: 3 grams
Protein: 0 grams
Cholesterol: 0 milligrams
Sodium: 1 milligram
Dietary Fiber: 0 grams

Carrot Cake

(This recipe also makes great muffins! You can eat them for breakfast or have them as a snack. They freeze great too.)

1 1/2 cups whole wheat flour	1 cup finely grated carrots
1 cup rolled oats	1 (8-ounce) can juice-packed crushed pineapple, drained
1 1/2 teaspoons baking soda, divided in half	
1 1/2 teaspoons cream of tartar	1/3 cup boiling water
2 teaspoons cinnamon	1/3 cup chopped dates
1 cup brown rice syrup	1/2 cup chopped pecans (optional)
2 teaspoons vanilla	
3 egg whites, unbeaten	Vanilla Frosting (see recipe)

Combine flour, oats, and 3/4 teaspoon baking soda, cream of tartar, and cinnamon in large mixing bowl. Mix well and set aside.

Combine next 5 ingredients; mixing well. Stir into flour mixture until flour is just moistened.

Blend in blender or food processor boiling water, dates, and other 3/4 teaspoon baking soda. Blend until pureed. <u>Gently</u> stir into flour mixture.

Spoon batter into two 9-inch round cake pans that have been sprayed with vegetable cooking spray and dusted with flour.

Bake at 350 degrees for 45-55 minutes. (Cake layers are done when they pull away from sides of the pan or when knife inserted in center comes out clean.) Cool for 15-20 minutes and remove layers from pans.

Frost layers with Vanilla Frosting and sprinkle top with chopped pecans.

Yield: 16 servings

Per Serving:

Calories: 143	Fat: 1 gram
Carbohydrate: 31 grams	Protein: 4 grams
Cholesterol: 0 milligrams	Sodium: 154 milligrams
Dietary Fiber: 2 grams	

Mandarin Orange Cake

1 cup boiling water
2 cups chopped dates, packed
1 1/2 teaspoons baking soda
1/2 cup fresh orange juice
1 cup unsweetened applesauce
1 cup brown rice syrup
1 cup egg beaters

1 teaspoon vanilla
2 1/4 cups whole wheat flour
1 teaspoon sea salt
1 teaspoon cinnamon
1 small can mandarin oranges, well drained
Grated rind of 1 large orange

Combine water, dates, and baking soda. Allow to soak until water cools.
Add orange juice and set aside.
Combine next 4 ingredients; mixing well.
Combine flour, salt, and cinnamon. Add to applesauce mixture.
Stir in soaked dates, orange rind, and mandarin oranges.
Spoon into bundt pan that has been sprayed with vegetable cooking spray and dusted with flour.
Bake at 350 degrees for 1 hour and 15 minutes or until knife inserted in center comes out clean.
Yield: 16 servings

Per Serving:
Calories: 182
Fat: 1 gram
Carbohydrate: 41 grams
Protein: 5 grams
Cholesterol: 0 milligrams
Sodium: 293 milligrams
Dietary Fiber: 4 grams

Millet Fruit Pudding

2-3 fresh strawberries, sliced
1/2 cup crushed pineapple, drained and juice reserved
1/2 teaspoon vanilla
3/4 cup hot millet
1/2 cup reserved pineapple juice
Dash sea salt
1 tablespoon raisins
6 raw almonds, chopped

Layer sliced strawberries on the bottom of a clear glass serving dish.

Blend next 5 ingredients in blender until consistency resembles pudding. (Add more reserved pineapple juice if necessary.)

Pour pudding over strawberry slices.

Sprinkle with nuts and raisins. Garnish with a whole fresh strawberry or kiwi slices if desired.

Yield: 1 serving

Per Serving:
Calories: 493
Fat: 6 grams
Carbohydrate: 94 grams
Protein: 10 grams
Cholesterol: 0 milligrams
Sodium: 33 milligrams
Dietary Fiber: 5 grams

Pina Colada Dessert Topping

1 (8-ounce) can unsweetened
    crushed pineapple, undrained
1 medium ripe banana, chopped
1/8 teaspoon rum flavoring
1/8 teaspoon coconut flavoring
2 tablespoons unsweetened flake coconut (optional)

Combine first 4 ingredients; chill well.
Serve over Vanilla Frozen Nonfat Yogurt. Sprinkle with coconut, if desired.
Yield: 1 cup

Per Tablespoon Serving:
Calories: 19
Fat: 0 grams
Carbohydrate: 5 grams
Protein: 0 grams
Cholesterol: 0 milligrams
Sodium: 0 milligrams
Dietary Fiber: 0 grams

Pumpkin Pie

3/4 pound "lite" firm tofu
2 cups canned or cooked pumpkin
2/3 cup brown rice syrup or honey
1 teaspoon vanilla
1 1/2 teaspoon ground cinnamon
3/4 teaspoon ground ginger
1/4 teaspoon ground nutmeg
1/4 teaspoon ground cloves
1 egg white
1 unbaked 9" deep-dish pie crust

Blend tofu in a food processor or blender until smooth.

Add next 7 ingredients and blend well. Pour into mixing bowl.

Beat egg white until soft peaks form. Fold gently into pumpkin mixture.

Pour into unbaked deep-dish pie shell.

Bake at 350 degrees for 1 hour. (Filling will be soft, but will firm up as it cools.)

Chill and serve.

Yield: 8 servings

Per Serving:
Calories: 243
Fat: 5 grams
Carbohydrate: 39 grams
Protein: 8 grams
Cholesterol: 0 milligrams
Sodium: 144 milligrams
Dietary Fiber: 2 grams

Raspberry-Peach Dessert Topping

1 (6-ounce) can frozen unsweetened apple juice concentrate thawed and undiluted
1 cup water, divided
2 cups chopped fresh peaches
3 tablespoons cornstarch
1/4 teaspoon almond extract
1 cup fresh raspberries

Combine apple juice concentrate, 2/3 cup water, and peaches in heavy saucepan. Cook over medium heat about 5 minutes or until peaches are tender.

Combine remaining 1/3 cup water and cornstarch; stir into peach mixture, and bring to a boil. Cook 1 minute, stirring constantly.

Remove from heat; stir in almond extract, and cool. Stir in raspberries before serving.

Serve over Frozen Vanilla Nonfat Yogurt.

Yield: 3 1/2 cups

Per Tablespoon Serving:
Calories: 11
Fat: 0 grams
Carbohydrate: 3 grams
Protein: 0 grams
Cholesterol: 0 milligrams
Sodium: 1 milligram
Dietary Fiber: 0 grams

Strawberry-Banana Dessert Topping

2 tablespoons cornstarch
1/8-1/4 teaspoon ground coriander
2 cups unsweetened apple juice
1 tablespoon honey
1 cup sliced strawberries
1 medium-sized ripe banana, sliced

Combine cornstarch and coriander in a small saucepan. Slowly stir in apple juice and honey.

Cook over medium heat until thick, stirring constantly. Remove from heat; let cool.

Fold in strawberries and banana just before serving. Serve over nonfat Vanilla Frozen Yogurt.

Yield: 2 1/2 cups

Per Tablespoon:
Calories: 13
Fat: 0 grams
Carbohydrate: 3 grams
Protein: 0 grams
Cholesterol: 0 milligrams
Sodium: 0 milligrams
Dietary Fiber: 0 grams

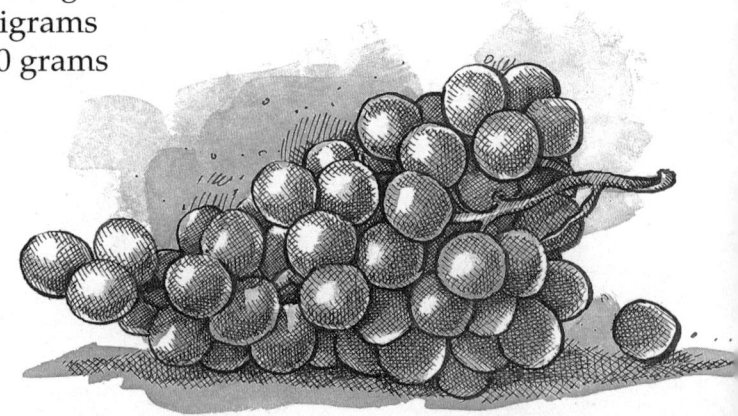

Vanilla Frosting

1 cup nonfat yogurt "cream" cheese
   (see recipe on page 135)
1/4-1/2 cup brown rice syrup,*
   (maple syrup may be used)
3 tablespoons nonfat milk powder*
2 teaspoons vanilla

Combine and beat together yogurt cheese, brown rice syrup, milk powder, and vanilla in chilled mixing bowl until well blended.
*Note: I start with 1/4 cup brown rice syrup and add as needed to get the consistency and sweetness I want. I also add more milk powder if needed to thicken.
   Yield: 1 1/2 cups (24 servings)
   (enough to frost two 9-inch layers or 1 bundt cake)

Per Serving:
Calories: 26
Fat: 0 grams
Carbohydrate: 4 grams
Protein: 1 gram
Cholesterol: 0 milligrams
Sodium: 20 milligrams
Dietary Fiber: 0 grams

Index

Animal Fats 11
Appetizers & Snacks 21
    Ants on a Log 24
    Appetizing Chicken Wontons 25
    Bagel Chips 26
    Banana Boats 27
    Banana-Yogurt Popsicles 28
    Crispy Tortilla Bowls 29
    Corn Tortilla Chips 30
    Crispy Rice Bars 31
    Date-Filled Wonton Tarts 32
    Fruitsicles 33
    Fruit Kabobs 34
    Herbed Pita Chips 35
    Millet-Spinach Appetizers 36
    Orange-Yogurt Popsicles 37
    Raggedy Anne Salad 38
    Strawberry Sorbet Pops 39
    Suckers 40
Breakfasts & Beverages 41
    Almond Milk 43
    Banana Milkshake 44
    Banana Pancakes 45
    Banana Smoothie 46
    Breakfast Bars 47
    Holiday "Eggnog" 48
    Holiday Wassail 50
    Hot Apple Punch 49
    Mexican Omelet 55
    Oatmeal Snacks 51
    Orange Pancakes 52
    Orange Pancake & Waffle Syrup 54
    Outstanding Oats 53
    Pineapple Cooler 56
    Spiced Breakfast Millet 57
    Strawberry Pancakes 58
    Weekend Breakfast Quiche 59
    Whole Wheat Waffles 60
Charts 172, 176, 199

Cooking
    Cooking Time for Beans & Legumes 199
    Cooking Time for Chicken & Turkey 233
    Cooking Time for Fish 221
    Cooking Time for Grains 176
Dairy Products 10
Dressings, Sauces, Spreads
                         & Dips 113
    Apple Butter 115
    Basil Vinaigrette Dressing 116
    Black Bean Salsa 117
    Black Bean Sauce 118
    Chickpea Sandwich Spread 119
    Garbanzo-Carrot Vegetable Spread 120
    Fat-Free Dill Dressing 121
    Fresh Fruit Dip 122
    Fresh Vegetable Dip 123
    Garlic Bean Dip 124
    Homemade Ketchup 125
    Honey Dijon Dressing 126
    Low-Fat Creamy Italian Dressing 127
    Low-Fat Vinaigrette 128
    Low-Fat Ranch 129
    Marinara Sauce 130
    Orange Pancake & Waffle Syrup 131
    Orange-Yogurt Fruit Dip 132
    Quick Pizza Sauce 133
    Spinach Dip 134
    Yogurt "Cream" Cheese 135
Fish 219
    Dilled Salmon 222
    Grilled Garlic-Basil Grouper 223
    Lemon-Dill Fish 224
    Orange Orange Roughy 225
    Orange Roughy Over Basil Vegetables 226
    Salmon Patties 227
    Tex-Mex Fillets 228
    Super Grouper with Orange Sauce 229
Grains 173, 174, 175

INDEX

Grains & Side Dishes 169
- Almond Wild & Brown Rice 178
- Barley Casserole 179
- Barley-Vegetable Pilaf 180
- Basil Brown Rice 181
- Brown Rice Pilaf 182
- Carrot-Rice Casserole 183
- Colorful Stuffed Peppers 184
- Italian Baked Rice 185
- Lemon-Dill Rice 186
- Mandarin Orange Millet 187
- Mexican Rice 188
- Millet Stuffed Squash 189
- Millet Supreme 190
- Orange-Herb Rice 191
- Quinoa & Squash Casserole 192
- Spinach & Rice Casserole 193
- Sweet Brown & Wild Rice with Sugar Snaps & Sweet Peppers 194
- Tomato-Millet Casserole 195

Nuts & Seeds 23

Poultry 231
- Basil Barley Chicken 234
- Chicken & Barley Casserole 235
- Chicken & Pepper Stir-Fry with Almonds 236
- Chicken Chili 237
- Chicken in Foil 238
- Chicken Fajita Pita Pockets 239
- Chicken-Rice Salad 240
- Honey-Mustard Chicken 241
- Lemon-Basil Chicken Tenders 242
- Pepper Chicken & Rice 244
- Quinoa & Chicken 246
- Stuffed Turkey Tenderloins 247
- Turkey Chili 248

Red Meats 7

Salads 95
- Black Bean & Barley Salad 97
- Carrot-Raisins Salads 98
- Citrus Marinated Fruit 99
- Orange Cabbage-Carrot Salad 103
- Colorful Brown Rice Salad 100
- Crunchy Barley Salad 101
- Marinated Fresh Fruit Bowl 102
- Orange Cabbage-Carrot Salad 103
- Rio Grande Quinoa & Corn Salad 104
- Salmon Pasta Salad 105
- Salmon & Wild Rice Salad 106
- Southwest Marinated Bean Salad 107
- Sunshine Spinach Salad 108
- Sweet Slaw 109
- Tomato-Basil Couscous Salad 110
- Tomato-Cucumber Salad with Dill Dressing 111
- Vegetable Pasta Salad 112

Soups 75
- Best-Ever Chicken & Rice Soup 77
- Broccoli Bisque 78
- Cabbage Soup 79
- Easy Black Bean Soup 80
- Great 9 Bean Soup 81
- Lentil-Barley Soup 82
- Lentil-Rice Soup 83
- Luscious Lentil Soup 84
- Minestrone Soup 85
- Fat-Free Chicken Broth 86
- Potato-Bean Soup 87
- Potato Leek Soup 88
- Potato-Yogurt Soup 89
- Spinach-Lentil Soup 90
- Tomato-Rice Soup 91
- Vegetable Barley Soup 92
- Vegetable Stock 93

Special Sweet Treats 249
    Almond Rice Pudding 252
    Apple Cake 253
    Apple Pie Dessert Topping 254
    Blueberry Dessert Topping 255
    Carrot Cake 256
    Mandarin Orange Cake 257
    Millet Fruit Pudding 258
    Pina Colada Dessert Topping 259
    Pumpkin Pie 260
    Raspberry-Peach Dessert Topping 261
    Strawberry-Banana Dessert Topping 262
    Vanilla Frosting 263

Sweetbreads, Muffins & Cookies 61
    Almond Raspberry Tortes 63
    Applesauce Muffins 64
    Applesauce-Raisin Bread 65
    Best-Ever Bran Muffins 66
    Chewy Apple-Oat Bars 67
    Cranberry Muffins 68
    Julie's Gingerbread 69
    Lemon Biscuits 70
    Oatmeal Banana Cookies 71
    Oatmeal Raisin Cookies 72
    Orange Muffins 73
    Sweet Corn Muffins 74

Sweeteners 251

Vegetarian Main Dishes 197
    Barley-Bulgur Vegetable Casserole 200
    Barley Vegetable Chili 201
    Black Bean Burritos 202
    Broccoli & Sun-Dried Tomatoes
      with Linguine 203
    Easy Spinach Lasagna 204
    Eggplant-Couscous Rolls 205
    Family Favorite Low-Fat Pizza 206
    Grain Burgers 207
    Grain Roast 208
    Italian Vegetable Pie 209
    Laura's Lentil Stew 210

Vegetarian Main Dishes (continued)
    Pasta Faggioli 211
    Mexican Pizza 212
    Pasta Madelena 213
    Pita Pizza 214
    Rice-Stuffed Eggplant 215
    Spinach-Basil Pasta 216
    Veggie Pita Pockets 217
    White Beans with Sage 218

Vegetable Side Dishes 137
    Apple Acorn Squash 139
    Apple Sweet Potatoes 140
    Baked Acorn Squash with Currant Sauce 141
    Baked Potato Croquettes 142
    CranApple Sweet Potatoes 143
    Dilled Asparagus 144
    Easy Stir-Fry Squash 145
    Elegant Eggplant Provencal 146
    Fresh Asparagus & Tomatoes 147
    Gala Garlic Potato Mash 148
    Grecian Green Beans 149
    Green Bean Bundles 150
    Green Beans with Pimento Strips 151
    Grilled Vegetables 152
    Lighter Potato Latkes 153
    Potato Gratin 154
    Sauteed Spinach & Garlic 155
    Sauteed Zucchini & Carrots 156
    Southern Corn Pudding in
      Tomato Cups 157
    Spiked Potatoes 158
    Squash & Onions 159
    Steamed Cauliflower, Carrots & Broccoli
      with Herb Sauce 160
    Steamed Garlic Broccoli 161
    Stuffed Baked Sweet Potatoes 162
    Sweet Carrots 163
    Sweet Sauteed Sugar Snaps 164
    Vegetable Medley 165
    Zucchini Fans 166
    Zucchini-Tomato Bake 167

INDEX